COGNITIVE BEHAVIOURAL THERAPY

COGNITIVE BEHAVIOURAL THERAPY

Your route out of **perfectionism**,

self-sabotage and

other everyday habits

AVY JOSEPH

CAPSTONE

Other Wiley Editorial Offices
John Wiley & Sons Inc., 111 River Street, Hoboken, NJ 07030, USA
Jossey-Bass, 989 Market Street, San Francisco, CA 94103-1741, USA
Wiley-VCH Verlag GmbH, Boschstr. 12, D-69469 Weinheim, Germany
John Wiley & Sons Australia Ltd, 42 McDougall Street, Milton, Queensland 4064, Australia
John Wiley & Sons (Asia) Pte Ltd, 2 Clementi Loop #02-01, Jin Xing Distripark, Singapore
129809
John Wiley & Sons Canada Ltd, 22 Worcester Road, Etobicoke, Ontario, Canada M9W 1L1

Wiley also publishes its books in a variety of electronic formats. Some content that appears in
print may not be available in electronic books.

A catalogue record for this book is available from the British Library and the Library of Congress.

ISBN 978-1-84112-800-9

Typeset by Sparks, Oxford – www.sparkspublishing.com
Printed and bound in Great Britain by TJ International Ltd, Padstow, Cornwall

Substantial discounts on bulk quantities of Capstone Books are available to corporations,
professional associations and other organizations. For details telephone John Wiley & Sons on
(+44) 1243 770441, fax (+44) 1243 770571 or email corporatedevelopment@wiley.co.uk

Contents

I wish to dedicate this book to the memory of my father who passed away three years ago.

Acknowledgements

Chris Hynes for unconditional love, help and support.

My family for the love and encouragement.

Professor Windy Dryden for his clinical and professional guidance.

Maggie Chapman for her friendship and professional support.

CHAPTER 1

Understanding CBT for goal achievement

'People are not disturbed by events but by the view they hold about them.'

Epictetus, Roman philosopher c. AD 75

This statement is probably the most important principle of Cognitive Behaviour Therapy (CBT): that of emotional responsibility.

This chapter will introduce you to some of the basic ideas and principles of Cognitive Behaviour Therapy (CBT) and how you can use it to help you achieve your goals. I'll be presenting the following topics:

- Basic principles
- Emotional responsibility
- Change is possible in the here and now
- Truth
- Common sense
- Helpfulness
- Types of thoughts
- Theory made simple

Basic principles

What does Cognitive Behaviour Therapy mean?

Cognitive simply means our 'thinking processes': how we think, how we acquire information and knowledge, how we store it in our head, how we evaluate it and how we base some of our decisions on it.

For example, how do you know that you are no good at drawing, singing, or mathematics? What made you form that opinion? Is it because you tried and realized that you couldn't draw, sing or work out equations? Is it because you received positive or negative feedback from other people? Did you come to your conclusion after one or several attempts? Did you know that you were good at drawing after making just one picture or that you were not good at singing after only one session? Perhaps it was only after repeatedly failing to get ten out of ten in mathematics that you began to believe that you couldn't do it.

When we make decisions, most of us think about whatever it is, then we think some more, and then again and again. We are thinking to ourselves most of the time. Does this thinking affect our opinion of ourselves and do these opinions affect how we feel? How do these opinions about ourselves influence our success?

Behaviour means our action or reaction to something. It's the doing bit. Our behaviour can be conscious or unconscious (out of our conscious awareness). In CBT, the word 'behaviour' comes from a branch of psychology called 'behaviourism', which is concerned with what can be observed rather than what can be speculated or assumed. It is based on what you have learned and become accustomed to, how this affects your actions and feelings, and how you can unlearn what you have learned in order to change.

Therapy means the treatment for a health problem, after a diagnosis or an assessment has been made.

CBT is a form of therapy that examines how our thinking, attitudes, beliefs, opinions and behaviour are formed, how they affect our success, our lives and feelings, and how changing them impacts on our performance. The ideas stem from both ancient and modern thinking in philosophy, science, psychology, common sense and humanity.

In this book I will show you how using CBT can help you set yourself up for success and overcome those beliefs and habits that sabotage your life. I am going to ask you to be open-minded and to consider whether changing your thinking, attitudes and beliefs about yourself and your abilities will affect your performance and your life.

Emotional responsibility

'People are not disturbed by events but by the view they hold about them.'

This principle is at the heart of nearly all emotional and behavioural change. It can be challenging because you may believe that it's what has happened to you that 'makes' you feel how you feel and do what you do.

Questioning this will show you that what you believe stops you from empowering yourself to move forward with your life. It will help you pursue your desired goals despite the obstacles and setbacks you may encounter in the process.

Is it true that events, situations or people make us feel what we feel?

First, let's look at the popular notion that your feelings are caused by events, situations or other people.

Think of a past event that caused you to respond with a certain emotion and associated actions. The only way you can change your feelings now is to wish that this event had not happened.

If someone else 'made' you feel and act in a certain manner, then the only way you can change your feelings now is to get that person from the past to change their feelings and take back whatever they did or said. And if that person is now dead, how can this be done?

Believing that the past, or a particular situation or person, causes feelings today, means that no one would ever be able to move forward or to change. We would all be totally stuck without any possibility or hope of ever altering anything. We would be slaves to the things that had happened to us or the people we had been involved with.

Can you imagine what it would be like if everyone felt hurt every time they experienced a rejection of some sort?

Rejection = Hurt
10 people rejected = 10 people feeling hurt
100 people rejected = 100 people feeling hurt
1000 people rejected = 1000 people feeling hurt

As an example, when you experience rejection you might feel hurt. If you believe that your feelings are caused by others, you may also believe that rejection only causes pain. This means that if you feel rejected no other feeling apart from hurt can be experienced. But don't some of us feel anger, sadness, depression, relief or happiness? If rejection only causes hurt then every person who has been rejected (that's probably all of us) would still be feeling hurt.

In fact, different people feel different emotions when they experience rejection:

Some people feel hurt
Some people feel angry
Some people feel depressed
Some people couldn't care less

Why do different people feel different things and what causes their feelings?

Is it true that events or people make us do what we do?

Let's think about what we do and assume that situations or people make us behave as we do.

A colleague criticizes you = You start avoiding them

If it is true that a colleague's criticism 'made' you avoid them, this means that every criticism made by your colleague would have the same effect on everyone. It means that avoidance is the only possibility whenever your colleague criticizes you, or anyone else for that matter.

A colleague criticizes 10 people = 10 people avoid them
A colleague criticizes 100 people = 100 people avoid them
A colleague criticizes 1000 people = 1000 people avoid them

Does this make sense?

The problem is that people say, 'he made me do it' or 'she made me lose my temper'. It is as if they have absolutely no control over how they feel or how they behave. Once again, if we do not have a part to play in how we feel and behave then we would be completely stuck, unable to move forward, learn or do anything useful. Is this what you see happening to everyone around you?

So what causes your feelings and reactions? Most of the time the simple answer is that you do. You cause your feelings and reactions by the way you think, the attitudes you've formed, the habits you no longer question and the beliefs you hold.

This is the principle of Emotional Responsibility: **You are largely responsible for the way you feel and act.**

The principle of emotional responsibility can be difficult to accept, particularly if you are going through a difficult time or have experienced trauma or personal tragedy. It's natural to feel angry, sad, depressed or hurt in response to accidents, illness and other challenges in life, but you can change your reactions after the initial feelings have passed.

Different people feel and experience contrasting emotions even when they go through the same tragedy. We all react differently to the same situation or event, or to what other people do or say. It is not the situation but your response that causes your emotions.

The thought manifests as the word;
The word manifests as the deed;
The deed develops into habit;
And habit hardens into character;
So watch the thought and its ways with care. (Buddha)

The way you think about something affects how you feel and how you behave. Here is an example:

- If you think that your partner's late arrival for dinner proves that you are not lovable then you might feel hurt and sulk.
- If you think that your partner was nasty and selfish because they arrived late for dinner then you might feel angry and shout.
- If you think that your partner's late arrival for dinner is no big deal then you can feel calm about it and ask what happened.

This shows that it is not the situation or what happens to us that causes our feelings and behaviour. It is the way we think about the situation. The way we think about something can then influence how we behave.

Change is possible in the here and now

The principle of emotional responsibility is not only true but also enormously empowering. It clearly shows us that we can change how we feel and act, if we want to. It shows that change is possible in the here and now. It shows that we can free ourselves from negative and unhelpful thinking patterns and behaviour. It shows that we are not slaves to the past, even if the things that happened were very bad.

Exercise

List five things that people manage to change about themselves despite doing it badly at first (for example, learning to drive).

1.

2.

3.

4.

5.

List five positive things that you have learned in your life despite experiencing difficulties (for example, moving on from a failed relationship).

1.

2.

3.

4.

5.

Think of an inspirational person (alive or dead) who has overcome enormous obstacles by having a powerful and constructive attitude and positive behaviour.

Truth

In CBT we examine out thoughts and behaviours to check if they are realistic. This means we judge and evaluate an event based on facts rather than our own or another person's version. Why do you think that, when an accident occurs, the police take statements from a number of people instead of asking just one person what happened?

Truth is about being consistent with reality. It's about striving for the goals that are important to you whilst also accepting, and not allowing yourself to be crippled by, the negative possibilities that exist in reality. It's about accepting the possibility that you may not get what you want while persisting in your efforts to reach your goals.

Exercise

How many 'F's can you count in the following statement?

FINISHED FILES ARE THE RESULTS OF YEARS OF SCIENTIFIC STUDY COMBINED WITH THE EXPERIENCE OF MANY YEARS.

Did you see 2 or 3 'F's?

There are 6.

I will leave you to find the rest but simply draw your attention to the word 'of'.

The above sentence is a well known example used to highlight the fact that we don't necessarily see the whole truth. We interpret what we see and experience. What you have learnt from this simple but effective exercise is that your version of the truth can be faulty. It is important to question the truth that you accept about yourself and your ability just in case you are seeing only a few of the good things and missing lots of others. Sometimes we only see a few 'F's, when in reality there are more. If the 'F's represent your positive abilities and qualities, how many of the good qualities are you seeing?

This is just one of the reasons why in CBT we question the validity or reality of our thoughts.

Common sense

In CBT we suggest taking a logical and common-sense approach to thinking.

This does not mean that you become totally unfeeling and emotionless.

Logic or common sense is about whether one statement connects logically to another.

For example, which one of these two statements makes sense?

A *Some men shave their heads … therefore anyone with a shaved head is a man.*

B *Some men shave their heads … but it doesn't mean everyone with a shaved head is a man.*

Clearly statement B makes sense. In statement A, the fact that some men shave their heads does not connect logically to the assumption that anyone with a shaved head is a man. Some women, children and teenagers also have shaved heads.

Logical thinking is useful because we all have the ability to think and use common sense. In CBT, using your common sense well can lead you to form better conclusions about yourself.

Some people think like this about certain goals:

I failed at achieving my goal   *therefore, I am a total failure as a person*

Others think like this:

I failed at achieving my goal   *but that doesn't mean I am a total failure. I am fallible but worthy nevertheless. I will learn from my failure and improve.*

Which of the above two statements makes more sense?

Helpfulness

Finally, in CBT we look at how helpful your thoughts are to you. Your thoughts are responsible for how you feel about yourself and your abilities so it is more useful for you to have more constructive and goal oriented thoughts than ones like those in the first example above.

This does not mean telling lies about your abilities and skills. If you told yourself lies then you wouldn't be operating in a realistic way.

Exercise

Reflect on some thoughts you often have about yourself and your abilities. See if they are helpful to you. For example, you might think 'I'm not very good at spelling'.

How can you make your thoughts more realistic, logical and helpful? For example, 'I could improve my spelling by going to school'.

Types of thoughts

In CBT we draw a distinction between different types of thoughts. Not all of our thoughts are involved with our feelings and behaviours. The thoughts that are involved in our feelings tend to have some sort of an assumption or judgement about ourselves, others or the world.

There are two particular types of thought which are involved in our emotions or feelings.

Inferences

Inferences are assumptions you make about reality that are important to you. These inferences can be about yourself, others or about the world. For example, if you were sitting in a meeting that was important to you and your boss contradicted you, you might think, 'he is undermining me'. Then you would be making an inference. This means that in that moment you have gone beyond the facts and made an assumption about what happened because it was significant to you. In this example you would have an emotional response: you may feel annoyed, concerned, very anxious, angry or enraged.

The question is whether your boss was undermining you or simply expressing a different opinion. In order to find out you would need to gather more information and evidence. Some of our inferences are accurate and some are not. In this example your inference has not been tested in reality.

If you had thought 'he has a different opinion, he is not undermining me' then your emotional response would be different.

Which of the following thoughts will lead to an emotion?

1) I saw a woman getting on a bus.

2) My workmates are ignoring me.

3) I won't get the job, I'm useless.

Thoughts 2 and 3 will lead to an emotional reaction. The second thought is an inference. It may or may not be true. Your colleagues have been ignoring you – they may just have been very busy with work. You need more information to assess the accuracy of conclusion. But if you conclude that you were being ignored then you would have an emotional reaction.

The third thought also leads to an emotional response but it is more profound in its conclusion. 'I won't get the job, I'm useless' is an evaluative thought.

Evaluations or beliefs

Inferences are partially involved in causing emotions and feelings. Evaluations, on the other hand, are thoughts that are fully involved in causing emotions and feelings. When you have an evaluative thought you are making a judgement about yourself, about others, or about the world. For simplicity let's call evaluative thoughts 'beliefs'. These are fundamental in causing constructive feelings and helpful behaviours or destructive feelings and sabotaging behaviours.

If you judge yourself as 'useless' when you are thinking about applying for a job, this will cause you to have additional thoughts such as 'I won't get the job'. When you hold such a belief, you will probably feel anxious when you go for the interview. In a state of anxiety, you will probably not perform as well as you are capable of doing and the likelihood of you getting the job decreases dramatically.

Theory made simple

Putting these principles and philosophies into a theoretical model helps you to see more easily how feelings, different thoughts, behaviours and events all interact with one another.

The easiest is the 'ABC' model of emotional response.

'A' can be real or imaginary

'A' stands for 'Activating Event' or trigger. The trigger can be an actual event, such as losing someone or something important to you, or an imaginary one. It could also be an inference – a hunch – like imagining that someone is going to reject you before any rejection has taken place.

'A' can be external or internal

External events are things that happen outside of your body, for example:

- someone's death
- losing something
- being rejected
- failing at something
- experiencing an accident.

Internal events are triggers that happen inside your body, for example:

- thoughts
- images
- emotions

- fantasies
- memories
- bodily sensations.

'A' can be about the past, present or future

The event could be something that has happened in the past, something that is happening now or something that will happen in the future.

Key points to remember:

- 'A' can be an external past event that was real. For example, losing someone you loved.
- 'A' can be real, future and external. For example, making a speech at your friend's wedding next week.
- It is not the event itself that causes your emotions but what you tell yourself or what you infer about it *now* that causes your feeling.
- It's easy to assume that any event which causes a reaction must be the trigger or cause.

A	B	C
Past, Present, Future Real or Imaginary External or Internal		Feelings Behaviours Thoughts (Inferences) Symptoms

When the trigger happens at 'A', you feel, behave, think and experience symptoms. Because this happens quickly, you think 'A' causes 'C' (the consequences). So you may use expressions like 'he *made* me feel angry', or 'my job *makes* me depressed'. It is as if we are not responsible for our own emotions.

Remember the 100 and 1000 people example earlier?

What causes our feelings is the 'B' between 'A' and 'C'. The 'B' stands for 'Belief'. So it is your belief (evaluation) of what happened that causes your emotions, behaviours, thoughts and symptoms.

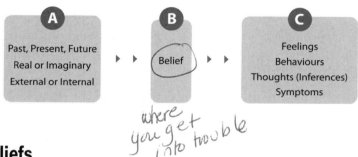

where you get into trouble

2 types ① healthy ② unhealthy

Beliefs

According to the ABC model we can have two types of belief – rational and irrational, healthy and unhealthy.

Healthy beliefs lead to emotional well-being and set you up for goal achievement.

Unhealthy beliefs lead to emotional disturbance and set you up for failure and goal sabotage.

Healthy beliefs

Healthy beliefs tend be flexible and are based on the things that you want, like, desire and prefer. They tend to make sense, they are logical and consistent with reality. This means accepting that sometimes you may not get what you want. A silly example of a flexible and realistic belief would be, 'I would like it to be nice and sunny every day when I wake up but I accept there is a chance that it might not be.'

If your belief system is healthy, you can accept yourself unconditionally whether or not you get what you want. Healthy beliefs detach human worth from success or failure. For example, 'I accept myself as a worth-while but fallible person regardless of whether I succeed or not. My worth does not depend on success.'

Unhealthy beliefs *Tyranny of the shoulds*

Unhealthy beliefs tend to be inflexible, rigid and dogmatic. They are based on 'MUST', 'HAVE TO', 'GOT TO', 'NEED TO', or 'ABSOLUTELY SHOULD'.

Rigid beliefs are inconsistent with reality. They don't accept other possibilities even though reality shows us that other possibilities exist. They cause a mismatch between internal and external realities. Take, for example, the thought, 'the day has to be nice and sunny when I wake up'. This is irrational and unhealthy because it just isn't possible. Unhealthy beliefs do not make logical sense. Just because 'I would like the day to be nice and sunny when I wake up', it does not follow that it 'HAS to be'.

Critical

If you are making a judgement about yourself, unhealthy beliefs tend to be self-critical. They also tend to be critical of others or the world in general. You might rate yourself as 'useless', 'unworthy', 'a failure' or 'unlovable'. You might believe that human worth depends on conditions or demands being met. This means you may think, 'if I fail, it proves that I'm a failure' or 'if people like me then I'm OK but if they don't approve of me it means I'm unworthy'.

Healthy negative emotions and self-helping behaviours

It is easy to understand that if you hold a healthy belief about yourself or about certain things in your life, this would increase your chances of success. However, success is never guaranteed, so if you don't succeed you might feel upset and sad. Having healthy beliefs means that, while you might feel nervous or concerned, you would lick your wounds, dust yourself off and focus back on your goal. Instead of feeling guilty you might feel regret and look at ways of improving. Instead of feeling unhealthy anger or rage, you might feel annoyed. You would behave assertively without lashing out in a destructive way or giving up because you see yourself as a failure.

There is a theme to the way you feel and behave. For example, when you feel anxious, it is because you think you are being threatened. In a state of anxiety, you feel as though you to want to escape or avoid the threat. The emotion is anxiety and the behaviour (what you want to do) is to run.

Unhealthy negative emotions and self-destructive behaviours

It is not difficult to understand that if you have unhealthy beliefs about yourself and about certain things in your life, your feelings and behaviours are not going to be healthy.

According to the ABC model, unhealthy beliefs cause unhealthy negative emotions and self-damaging or destructive behaviours. Depression, anxiety, guilt and rage are examples of unhealthy negative emotions caused by unhealthy irrational beliefs.

Anxiety vs concern

Unhealthy Negative Emotion	What the belief is about	Healthy Negative Emotion
Anxiety	A threat or danger	Concern
How you think		**How you think**
You exaggerate the overall effect of the threat		You keep the effect of the danger in perspective
You think that you won't be able to deal with the danger		You have a balanced view about your ability to deal with the threat
You see the glass as half empty		You see the whole glass and focus on the full part
Your thoughts are not constructive		Your thoughts are solution-focused and constructive
What you do or want to do		**What you do or want to do**
Run away physically		Face the threat
Run away mentally		Deal with the potential danger
Do superstitious things to get rid of the threat		
Medicate and numb your feelings e.g. with alcohol		
Seek assurances from others		

Do it afraid

Depression vs sadness

Unhealthy Negative Emotion	What the belief is about	Healthy Negative Emotion
Depression	**Loss or failure**	**Sadness**
How you think		**How you think**
You only focus on negatives since the loss or failure		You think of both the negatives and positives of the loss or failure
You think of all the other past losses and failures		You do not dwell on past losses and failures
You think you are a failure, helpless		You do not see yourself as a failure or as helpless. You think that you can help yourself to move forward
You think the future is hopeless, bleak and full of misery		You have hope for the future
What you do or want to do		**What you do or want to do**
You pull away from other people		You express how you feel about your loss or failure
You withdraw into your head		You look after yourself and your environment
You stop looking after yourself and your environment		You engage in healthy behaviours
You get rid of your emotions in destructive ways, e.g. alcohol or overeating		

Anger/rage vs annoyance

Unhealthy Negative Emotion	What the belief is about	Healthy Negative Emotion
Anger or rage	**Your rule has been broken, your self-esteem threatened or you experience frustration**	**Annoyance**
How you think		**How you think**
You exaggerate the actions of the person who has broken your personal rule		You are balanced about the intention behind the thing that was done
You think the other person's intentions were malicious		You don't see malice
You are right and the other person is definitely wrong		You are open to being wrong
You can't see the other person's point of view		You can listen to the other person's point of view
You think of how you can get your revenge		You do not think of seeking revenge
What you do or want to do		**What you do or want to do**
You physically attack		You talk and behave in an assertive manner but with the right intent
You verbally attack		
You pay them back somehow e.g. by ignoring them or staying silent		You ask the other person to make changes but you don't demand it
You recruit allies against the other person		

Hurt vs sorrow

Unhealthy Negative Emotion	What the belief is about	Healthy Negative Emotion
Hurt	Someone has treated you badly. You think you deserve to be treated better	Sorrow
How you think		**How you think**
You exaggerate the unfairness of your treatment		You think in a balanced way about the unfairness
You think the other person does not care about you		You do not think the other person does not care about you
You think of yourself as unlovable or misunderstood		You do not think of yourself as unlovable or misunderstood
You remember the other times when you felt hurt		You don't think about the other times when you felt hurt
The other person must understand and make amends first		You don't insist the other person has to make the first move
What you do or want to do		**What you do or want to do**
You sulk and shut down		You talk about how you feel in order to persuade the other person to behave more fairly
You pick on the other person without telling them why		

Guilt vs remorse

Unhealthy Negative Emotion	What the belief is about	Healthy Negative Emotion
Guilt	You have broken a moral code or the feelings of a significant person were hurt	Remorse
How you think		**How you think**
You have definitely committed a sin		You think about what you did and put it in context before you make a judgement
You think you are more responsible than another		You are balanced about your responsibility and the other person's
You forget about how things were		You acknowledged the situation and the circumstances before you did what you did
You deserve punishment		You don't think about retribution
What you do or want to do		**What you do or want to do**
You escape from your feeling in destructive ways		You face up to the healthy pain
You plead for forgiveness and/or punish yourself by physical deprivation		You ask for forgiveness but you do not physically punish yourself
You make unrealistic promises never to do it again		You make appropriate amends
You deny that you did anything bad		You accept your poor behaviour without making excuses

Shame vs regret

Unhealthy Negative Emotion	What the belief is about	Healthy Negative Emotion
Shame or Embarrassment	Something shameful has been revealed about you. Other people judge you or shun you	Regret
How you think		**How you think**
You exaggerate the shameful information revealed		You remain compassionate about yourself. You accept yourself
You exaggerate the likelihood of negative judgement		You are realistic about the likelihood of negative judgement
You think the negative judgement will last a long time		You are realistic about the length of negative judgement
You exaggerate the degree of negative judgement		You are realistic about the degree of negative judgement
What you do or want to do		**What you do or want to do**
Avoid eye contact with others		You continue participating in social events
Avoid others		You accept others' intervention to restore social harmony
Attack others who have shamed you		
Defend your ego in self defeating ways		
Ignore others who attempt to help restore balance		

Unhealthy envy vs healthy envy

Unhealthy Negative Emotion	What the belief is about	Healthy Negative Emotion
Unhealthy envy	**Another person has something you find desirable**	**Healthy envy**
How you think		**How you think**
You devalue the desired object		You admit to yourself that you too desire it
You tell yourself that you don't want it, even if you do		You admit that you'd also want it and accept that you do
You try to attain it, even if it is not useful to you		You find ways to attain it only because you want it
You put other people down and attempt to deprive them of the desired object		You do not put other people down and you allow them to enjoy it
What you do or want to do		**What you do or want to do**
You belittle the desired object verbally		You do not belittle the desired possession
You belittle the other person verbally		You attempt to attain it but only if you want it
You attempt to remove or deprive the other person from desired possession		
You spoil or destroy the desired object or possession		

Unhealthy jealousy vs healthy jealousy

Unhealthy Negative Emotion	What the belief is about	Healthy Negative Emotion
Unhealthy jealousy	**There is a potential threat to a relationship from another person**	**Healthy jealousy**
How you think		**How you think**
You see threat to your relationship when none exists		You do not see threat where none exists
You think infidelity will definitely happen		You do not think infidelity will definitely happen
You misinterpret your partner's conversation with and actions towards another as having sexual or romantic feelings		You do not misinterpret your partner's conversation with another as having sexual meaning
You have visual images of infidelity		You do not create sexual images of your partner with another
If your partner admits to finding someone attractive, you see yourself as less attractive		You accept that your partner can find another attractive without thinking that you are less attractive
You want your partner to only ever think of you		You accept that your partner can see others as attractive just as you can

Exercise

Identify the different emotions and work out if they are healthy or unhealthy.

Sam is a 40-year-old man and has been married for three years. He is studying towards some professional qualifications and has to sit his final exams in a couple of months. He is finding it difficult to concentrate when he sits down to revise. He keeps thinking that he will fail and, whenever he tries to revise, he ends up doing other work. When his wife tells him to sit down and get on with it he slams his books shut and shouts at her. After his outburst he ends up begging for forgiveness and thinks that he is a bad person.

Answer

Anxiety – unhealthy negative emotion
Anger – unhealthy reaction
Guilt – unhealthy

Exercise

Write about what it would be like if you held healthy rational beliefs about yourself and your abilities instead of unhealthy irrational ones.

How would you feel if you changed your beliefs to healthy ones?

What would you be able to do better and more successfully if you held healthy beliefs about yourself?

The diagram below illustrates key points in this chapter.

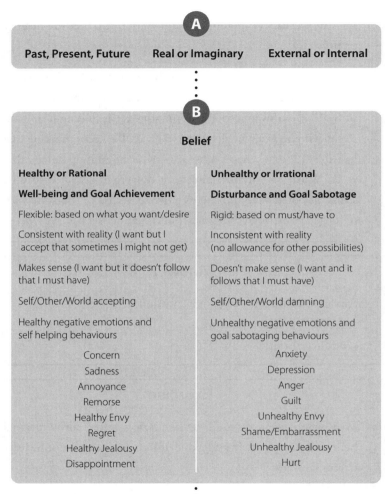

A

Past, Present, Future   Real or Imaginary   External or Internal

B

Belief

Healthy or Rational	**Unhealthy or Irrational**
Well-being and Goal Achievement	**Disturbance and Goal Sabotage**
Flexible: based on what you want/desire	Rigid: based on must/have to
Consistent with reality (I want but I accept that sometimes I might not get)	Inconsistent with reality (no allowance for other possibilities)
Makes sense (I want but it doesn't follow that I must have)	Doesn't make sense (I want and it follows that I must have)
Self/Other/World accepting	Self/Other/World damning
Healthy negative emotions and self helping behaviours	Unhealthy negative emotions and goal sabotaging behaviours

Concern	Anxiety
Sadness	Depression
Annoyance	Anger
Remorse	Guilt
Healthy Envy	Unhealthy Envy
Regret	Shame/Embarrassment
Healthy Jealousy	Unhealthy Jealousy
Disappointment	Hurt

C

Feelings   Behaviours   Thoughts (Inferences)   Symptoms

CHAPTER 2

Healthy and unhealthy beliefs

W hat makes our beliefs and thoughts healthy or unhealthy?

In this chapter, you will learn about healthy and unhealthy beliefs in more detail. Understanding the following concepts will help you to identify what makes beliefs and thoughts healthy or unhealthy.

Want to vs have to

Want to versus have to is at the heart of goal achievement. Understanding this concept will help you appreciate the difference between choice-based motivation and restrictive fear-based motivation. It will help you understand the effect of such attitudes on your mind and body and show that there are very few responses that you *have to* make. You always have choices, even if they are sometimes limited. *you always have a choice*

Bad vs awful

In your efforts to achieve your goals it is important to know how to evaluate the 'badness' you experience, and how to make judgements about things that don't work out as you want them to. Your mind and body respond in accordance with your evaluation, even if its flawed.

Difficult vs unbearable

We all experience problems in many areas of our lives but don't always realize that our minds and bodies respond to how we rate them. Evaluating a difficulty as unbearable is not only flawed but it also triggers images and feelings that fight against goal achievement.

Self-acceptance vs self-damning

Learning to rate your performance and actions on an individual level instead of comparing yourself to others will help you remain focused on your goal and your performance.

What you believe is based on the judgements you make. All of us make judgements and hold beliefs about ourselves, about other people and about the world.

Beliefs can be good, rational and healthy or bad, irrational and unhealthy. Your beliefs not only cause your feelings, they also influence the way that you think. Your decisions, opinions and attitudes are based on the beliefs that you hold about yourself. This in turn affects your performance and goal achievements.

If you hold a negative judgement or an unhealthy belief about yourself, you will feel an emotion based on that judgement. You will then have an opinion of yourself and your abilities based on your belief. Your performance will be limited by the consequences of your unhealthy belief.

The diagram shows how this can lead to a cycle, which can be either healthy and constructive or destructive and negative. If your belief about yourself is good, rational and healthy, your opinion of yourself, and your thoughts, decisions and attitudes, will be constructive. You will achieve stronger performance and success in your goals.

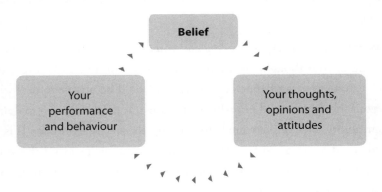

For example, you believe that if you study hard you will have the chance of getting a distinction. You also have a healthy attitude to failure. You believe that while failing to get a distinction would be very disappointing and difficult, you would not give up. Instead, you would learn from the situation and work harder next time.

This type of belief causes you to have positive thoughts and attitudes which will help you focus on your studies. They will enable you to relax, which in turn means that you will absorb and retain more information. With such a positive and helpful mental state your performance will improve and the probability of getting a distinction will be greater.

When you receive your results the possible scenarios are:

1) You get a distinction. This further improves and strengthens your thoughts and attitudes about your ability.
2) You don't get a distinction. You may feel disappointed and upset but then you focus on your studies again.

Your cycle of belief, thoughts and performance is dynamic, positive and strong.

If your belief is anxiety producing and you do not have a healthy attitude to failure, your thoughts will reflect that. If you think that failure is the worst thing that can happen and that you would be unable to deal with it, your thoughts would probably be negative. You would begin to doubt your ability and be distracted from doing the necessary work. This in turn could lead you to lose concentration and perhaps avoid the work altogether. The likelihood of failure or not getting a distinction in your examination would increase.

When you receive your results there are two possible scenarios:

1) You get a distinction. This means that next time you sit an exam you will still feel anxious because your belief about failing won't have changed. You are more likely to think you could fail and then the whole loop of anxious thoughts and behaviour will start again.
2) You don't get a distinction. You may feel as though it is all over for you and motivating yourself to sit the examination again will feel like a very daunting task. The self doubt and feelings of anxiety will increase.

The cycle of your unhealthy belief, thoughts and performance is static, negative and destructive.

I hope the above example may have given you some clues about what makes a belief healthy and constructive and what makes it unhealthy and sabotaging.

HEALTHY AND UNHEALTHY BELIEFS   33

What makes a belief good, rational and healthy?

In Chapter 1 you learned that a healthy belief is flexible, consistent with reality, logical and helpful to you in terms of goal achievement.

An unhealthy belief is rigid, inconsistent with reality, illogical and unhelpful to your well being and happiness.

Exercise

Look again at the above example and write down what you have learned about some of the concepts that make a belief healthy or unhealthy.

Write down what you learned about how an unhealthy belief affects thoughts and performance.

Write down what you learned about how a healthy belief affects thoughts and performance.

Healthy beliefs are at the core of psychological health and goal achievement and unhealthy beliefs are at the core of psychological disturbance and sabotage.

Want to vs have to

Most of us talk about what we 'want to' do and what we 'must do' without paying too much attention to the meaning behind these expressions and the feelings they cause. I want you to consider all the things that you feel are an absolute 'have to' in your life.

- Is it that you feel you 'have to' work?
- Could it be that you feel you 'have to' have love in your life?
- Maybe it's that you consider you 'have to' look after someone?
- Perhaps it's that you think you 'have to' achieve your dreams?

According to CBT, people have a tendency to take the things they want to achieve and turn them into demands. For example, a child learns to play the piano because she really enjoys playing and loves the sound. She begins to practise harder and rapidly improves. She gets praised and this in turn motivates her to do more. She then has the opportunity to perform in front of her friends at school and she knows that everyone will be there watching her. She really wants to do well and not make a mistake when she is playing in front of all those people. She begins to think, 'I'm going to practise harder to ensure that I don't make a mistake'. Her friends ask her 'How are you feeling about playing? Aren't you scared about making a mistake?' A teacher may say, 'I hope you're practising because you don't want to make a mistake' and so on. She then begins to put pressure on herself by thinking, 'I must make sure that I don't make a mistake'. By the time of the performance she is in a state of fear because she is now telling herself that she 'has to' get it right.

This simple example illustrates how you can turn your 'want to' into a stressful 'have to'. This is simply a human trait – we all have the ability to turn our desires and wants into dogmatic and absolute 'have to's. Other words for 'have to' are: must, need to, got to, absolutely should, ought to.

CBT believes that these demands are at the core of psychological disturbance and emotional problems. They cause us to feel unhealthy negative emotions such as anxiety, which in turn block creativity and limit our potential when it comes to goal achievement.

'Have to' and 'must' are rigid and inflexible

These inflexible demands that you impose on yourself, on other people or on the world, do not allow for the existence of other options such as not fulfilling your demand.

For example, if you make a demand such as 'I have to succeed' or 'I must not fail', you are not allowing for the possibility that you might not succeed.

You can clearly see that by operating in this rigid way you are essentially saying you do not have a choice. You are telling yourself, 'this is how it must be for me'.

Of course, some things do have to function in a certain way. The law of gravity means that if you drop a stone it will 'have to' fall down. We all 'have to' eat, drink, breathe and have shelter in order to survive. Otherwise we would die. And that is another 'have to' – we all 'have to' die at some point, whether we believe in an afterlife or not.

Most of the things that we believe are 'have to's are in fact wants or desires.

Exercise

List five important things in your life that you think you *have to* do.

Example: I have to go to work.

List five important things in your life that *have to* happen.

Example: I have to be happy.

List five important things in your life that *must not* happen.

Example: I must not be alone.

'Have to' and 'must' are not consistent with reality

'Have to' is not consistent with reality because in real life we sometimes do not get the things we insist on.

For example, if you hold the belief 'I must not make a mistake', you are essentially saying that it must happen. Reality shows that everyone makes mistakes. That is the truth and you cannot escape from it by avoiding it, denying it or burying it. That's how it is even if you really dislike it.

The same applies to other demands you may make, such as a 'have to' about other people's judgement of you: 'I have to be liked by people I meet'. Here reality will show you that while many people do like you, there will be some who might not. Insisting on being liked does not alter reality even if you hate it.

When you do not accept what the real world shows you, you are operating solely in your own internal world or your version of reality. You are living in your head and refusing to acknowledge the truth of how things are.

'Have to' and 'must' are not logical

'Have to' and 'must' are not logical or based on common sense. They do not rationally follow from what you want.

If you reason that because you want something therefore it must happen, you show very poor logic. It means everything that you want or desire HAS to happen. The interesting thing is that you probably have a lot of common sense but sometimes you may let go of it when it concerns something you really want. In such cases you make yourself more vulnerable to the impact of unhealthy reasoning.

If you apply logic to the above example, then your desire would be to do well and not make a mistake. This is fair enough. It is healthy for you to have your own dreams, wants and likes. However, it would not make sense for you to demand that you have to get things right or that you must not make a mistake just because it is what you want. This would be poor reasoning.

Example

Consider the statement below. You can see that it is made up of two parts. Part one is the statement about your desire for something. Let's call that something 'xyz'. The second statement is a conclusion that follows from your first statement.

I want xyz .... AND THEREFORE I MUST HAVE xyz

Now replace xyz with 'the day to be nice and sunny'. Does your second statement sound reasonable?

I want the day to be nice and sunny .... AND THEREFORE the day MUST be nice and sunny.

Replace xyz with 'to get things right', or any other desire, and the same logic will apply. It is irrational to make the second demanding statement as this does not allow for the numerous other possibilities.

'Have to' and 'must' are not helpful

When you make an unreasonable and unrealistic demand on yourself, you cause a lot of tension and stress in your body.

If you demand that the day must be nice and sunny despite the fact that reality is showing you other possibilities, then you are not in a state of balance. You are essentially trying to force reality to be different from what it is; you cannot be at peace with the laws of nature; you are blinding yourself to the truth. This causes you to be tense and uncomfortable, and have unhealthy feelings of anxiety, depression and guilt.

In such a state your thinking becomes more negative and your conclusions tend to be untrue, unreasonable and limiting. Your behaviour is influenced by all of this. You may feel shackled or forced into action. You may feel as if someone is pushing you instead of believing that you are in control and can make choices.

Example

Anne's goal is to feel confident and speak eloquently in staff meetings. She is anxious about whether she will remember what she wants to say when her turn comes to give an update to the rest of her colleagues. She tells herself, 'you've got to remember when your turn comes; you have to calm down'. Her thoughts are about trying to remember at the same time as she is looking and counting how many people are ahead of her.

She becomes more insistent with her self-demand and the pressure to remember starts growing. She is no longer focused, in the moment, attentive to what is being discussed. She is completely operating in her own head. She notices her feelings of anxiety and worry are growing and begins to tell herself that she has to calm down. This causes more tension and pressure. Her heart is now beating rapidly, her palms are sweating and what she wants to do is get out of the meeting.

Her unrealistic demands do not help her. They cause her feelings of anxiety. They cause her thoughts to be focused on herself rather than on the meeting. She monitors herself constantly checking when her turn is going to be. She feels her body experiencing the physical symptoms of anxiety and all she wants is for the meeting to stop.

Her demands do not help. They will not help her achieve her goal of speaking confidently and eloquently.

Bad vs awful

How you judge the things you consider as 'bad' makes a big difference to how you feel. When you don't get what you want, you may decide that is bad. This judgement can be healthy, rational, realistic and logical or it can be unhealthy, irrational, unrealistic and illogical.

CBT says that if you are *not* making a demand about the things you want, you will evaluate the badness of the situation in a realistic way that helps you move forward. However, if you *are* making a demand about what you want then you will evaluate or judge the badness in an unhealthy way that blocks you.

You look at the badness as if it is the worst thing that can happen to you or to any human being. This means you believe that nothing worse can happen. You may feel as if the world has ended. This is what we call 'Awfulizing' or 'Catastrophizing' the bad experience.

Think back to the example of the child who plays the piano: you will recall that her demand is that she must not make a mistake when she performs in front of her friends. Because she is demanding something from her internal world that excludes the reality of making a mistake, it stands to reason that she may then view making a mistake as bad. Let's assume that she goes a step further and believes that making a mistake during her performance is the worst thing that can happen to her. She is now awfulizing. In her view there is nothing worse than making a mistake and she now operates with this belief.

Of course, not everyone will see making a mistake as 'the end of the world'. However, there are certain events or some possibilities that you might feel are the worst things that might happen. This will affect how you feel, how you think and how you behave. All of these will influence your performance and potential to achieve your goals in a healthy way.

In CBT, awfulizing beliefs cause unhealthy negative emotions and self-sabotaging behaviours.

Awfulizing beliefs are rigid and inflexible

When you see something as the worst possible thing that might happen, you are not allowing for the possibility that, actually, worse things can happen.

For example, if you believe you have to succeed because if you don't it would be awful, or even the end of the world, you are not allowing for the possibility that worse things than failure can happen.

You can see that making this sort of judgement about the badness of not succeeding is inflexible and rigid.

Nothing is the-end-of-the-world bad – apart from the end of the world itself, of course. For everything you believe is the worst possible scenario, I could suggest something worse. For everything I may view as the worst thing that could happen, you could suggest something worse. This concept could be controversial as you may be thinking of something very emotive, but when you allow yourself time to reflect, you will probably realize that there is always the possibility of something even worse – for example, the end of the world itself.

Exercise

List five important things in your life that you would view as the end of the world or the worst thing that could happen, for example failing at something.

Awfulizing beliefs are not consistent with reality

It is not consistent with reality to see something as the worst thing that could happen. Clearly, something even worse could happen. You cannot prove that a worse thing could not happen. If you hold the belief 'I must not make a mistake because making a mistake would be awful' i.e. the worst thing that could happen, you are essentially saying that nothing worse than that is possible. If this was true, the world would have ended a long time ago because making a mistake would have been worse than a volcanic eruption.

Reality shows you that the world hasn't ended despite the fact that you made a mistake. So while making a mistake may be bad for you and possibly even for other people, it is still not the worst thing that might happen.

You may argue that to you it *is* the worst thing that could happen. But think about how that alters your actual reality. What consequences does it have for your life and performance?

When you do not accept what external reality shows you, you are once again operating in your own internal world or internal reality. You are living in your head and shutting yourself off from the truth.

This doesn't mean denying that bad things do happen, but remember not to turn that badness into the end of the world.

Awfulizing beliefs are not logical

It does not make sense to catastrophize the things you view as bad. You may think, 'well, I'm not logical and that's just me' or, 'if I want to make something the worst thing then I will'. You have every right to think exactly as you wish. You may think in a reasoned and logical way about the bad things or you may think in the opposite way – that is your choice. Your conclusions and reasoning can be right or wrong. That reasoning will impact on how you feel and perform.

You may understand logic and reasoned thinking but when you let go of it, you may find you are vulnerable to reasoning in unhealthy and wrong ways about your situation, yourself and your abilities.

Example

The statement below is made up of two parts. Part one acknowledges that something is bad. Let's call that something 'xyz'. The second statement makes a conclusion that follows from the first statement.

Xyz is bad .... AND THEREFORE xyz is the end of the world (or awful, or terrible, or a catastrophe; the worst thing possible).

Now if you replaced xyz with 'a rainy cold day', does your second statement sound reasonable?

A rainy cold day is bad .... AND THEREFORE a rainy cold day is the end of the world.

Replace xyz with 'making a mistake', and the same logic will apply. Logically it is wrong to make a catastrophic conclusion from the first part of the statement.

Awfulizing beliefs are not helpful

If you turn the badness of an event or a possible event into the worst thing that has happened or could happen, this awfulizing evaluation will cause you to feel a lot of tension and stress. If you view something as terrible or awful, you will experience unhealthy negative emotions like anxiety, rage or guilt. Your body responds to what you believe whether it is true or not, so if you believe making a mistake is terrible you will feel anxious about making mistakes. In this state of anxiety your thoughts will be negative and your behaviour will follow. You cannot expect to be at your best when you are thinking the worst thing in the world, i.e. making a mistake, is a possibility.

This can create a circular loop in your thinking, for example, 'it would be awful if I made a mistake and so I must not make a mistake' or, 'I must get things right because it would be terrible if I didn't'. As a result, you will be watching and waiting to make a mistake.

Awfulizing in this way causes you to have thoughts and feelings that are unhealthy. It limits what you can achieve and creates harmful physiological symptoms.

Example

Let's go back to the earlier example of the woman whose goal is to feel confident and speak eloquently in staff meetings. She feels anxious about remembering what she wants to say. She imposes a demand on herself to remember because she views going blank as the worst thing that could happen to her. She continues to insist that she has to remember because if she doesn't it would be awful, even catastrophic. She feels the anxiety caused by both the demand she is making and by the fact that she sees going blank not just as bad but as TERRIBLE. As she notices her anxiety she starts to demand that she MUST calm down: 'Oh, I'm anxious, this is horrible. I MUST calm down'. This in turn produces even more anxiety.

She is looking around at her colleagues and all her thoughts are about how *terrible* it would be if she didn't remember and how *awful* it will be if she can't calm herself down in time. She is now in a state of desperation and all her body wants to do is to get out of that meeting room. She is totally engaged in her catastrophic thoughts and in her own head. Her pulse is racing and she can feel the blood pressure rising.

Her rigid and catastrophizing belief will not help her achieve her goal of confident and eloquent speech.

There are, of course, times when anxiety is healthy. For example if our lives are in real danger, anxiety causes adrenaline to pump through our bodies to prepare for the fight or flight. So if making a mistake is believed to be life-threatening, the body will react in the same way: with anxiety and fear.

Difficult vs unbearable

What you tell yourself about the things you either find or imagine you find difficult affects how you feel and influences to a great degree the choices you make. It impacts how you think and behave and ultimately affects your performance. Let's look more closely at the things you find difficult.

If you think about the things you find difficult as opposed to bad, you may judge many things that have happened or could happen as both bad and difficult.

When you don't get what you want or desire or when you think about not getting what you want and desire, you may judge that as difficult, for example, when you don't get your own way or when you cannot resolve a problem immediately. How you judge such difficulties can be either healthy or unhealthy. A healthy judgement will tend to be rational, logical and realistic. An unhealthy judgement will tend to be irrational, unrealistic and illogical.

When you are *not* making a demand about what you want, your judgement of what you find difficult will be realistic, healthy and problem-solving, and will help you to move forward. However, if you make a demand about what you want, your judgement of its difficulty will be unhealthy and unhelpful; it will make you feel stuck. Remember that demands make you feel as if you do not have any choice at all, causing you to feel as if you are being forced into doing something.

In effect, you make the difficulty 'unbearable'. You will probably use expressions like 'I can't cope', 'I can't stand it', 'it's unbearable'. In CBT we call this a 'Low Frustration Tolerance' (LFT) belief. You believe you are not capable of bearing the frustration or the difficulty of not getting what you are demanding.

Think back to the example of the child who plays the piano. She was already causing herself considerable anxiety by demanding that she absolutely must not make a mistake during her performance. Her body and mind were operating as if someone was forcing her to play the piano in front of her friends. In such a state, it is easy to understand that not only is she catastrophizing, but also that making a mistake would be UNBEARABLE to her. In her view making a mistake would be something she would not be able to tolerate or stand. This third belief about not tolerating mistakes causes further anxiety and adds to her worries.

It is possible that you have all three unhealthy beliefs about certain things in your life. For example, you may make a demand about how certain people drive on the road; you may tell yourself it's awful that they drive that badly and how unbearable you find it. This type of thinking can cause irrational anger or even road rage. You may view bad driving as terrible but tolerate it. Or you may not find it terrible but definitely feel like you cannot stand it. In other words you may have both the catastrophizing belief and the LFT about certain things, or you may just have one of them, as a result of your demands. LFT beliefs cause unhealthy negative emotions, thoughts and self sabotaging behaviours.

LFT beliefs are rigid and inflexible

When you make the difficulty or frustration you are experiencing 'unbearable' or 'intolerable', you are not allowing for the possibility – or even the fact – that you can tolerate it, or indeed that you are tolerating it.

For example, if you hold the belief 'I have to succeed because if I don't it will be unbearable' then you are not allowing for the fact that you have accepted it and still are tolerating it.

You can easily see that believing you cannot stand or tolerate something is inflexible and rigid. When you think about it, believing something is unbearable does not leave you any room for improvement. Your body's responses, emotions, thoughts and behaviour will be a consequence of what you tell yourself about the difficulty.

Exercise

List five important things in your life that you believe were unbearable for you, for example: it was unbearable when my relationship ended.

List five important things that you believe you would not be able to cope with, for example: I couldn't cope with confrontation.

Despite the fact that you have felt some things were unbearable, you are still here, reading this. What does this fact tell you about your resiliency?

LFT beliefs are not consistent with reality

It is not consistent with reality to believe that something is unbearable when you are still here to talk about it. When you tell yourself something is intolerable or unbearable you almost believe that you would cease to exist if that situation or event actually happened. If you see things that won't kill you as unbearable, you are telling yourself that you will die even though it is not true.

For example, if you hold the belief, 'I must not make a mistake because making a mistake would be unbearable', i.e. I will die, this means that mistakes are something you could not survive. If this were true, none of us would be alive because we have all made mistakes.

Reality shows that you do tolerate making mistakes even if you find it very hard to do so. Reality shows that you still manage to get up, make a cup of tea, shower, do your work and carry on functioning. It shows that as long as you are alive and breathing you can cope with the thing that you have been telling yourself is unbearable. I have had many clients who initially believed that going through a divorce was unbearable but they survived it. We convince ourselves of these things, even if they are not true, instead of reminding ourselves of the reality and the truth about our strength and resilience in tolerating difficulties.

When you do not focus on reality and tell yourself that how you feel is a true reflection of the facts, you are operating on your version of the truth and in your own internal world. You close yourself to the truth.

If you are going through a difficult time right now, acknowledge that you are experiencing difficulties and frustrations. But do not give up on the reality that you *are* tolerating whatever is happening, proved by the fact that you are still alive and reading this book.

LFT beliefs are not logical

It is not logical to conclude that something is unbearable just because it is very or even extremely difficult when you are still alive and breathing. Your feelings will come from such conclusions. This is important to think about, because sometimes faulty thinking becomes so effortless and habitual that you just accept it without question. You do not have to like logic but it is in your best interest to use common sense. You have lots of common sense and it is going to be up to you to identify your faulty thinking because there is something in it for you.

Example

Consider the statement below. You can see that it is made up of two parts. Part one acknowledges that something is difficult or frustrating. Let's call that difficulty 'xyz'. The second statement is about the conclusion that follows from the first statement.

Xyz is difficult .... AND THEREFORE xyz is unbearable (or intolerable, or I can't stand it or I can't cope with it).

When you replace the xyz with 'a rainy, cold day', does the second statement sound reasonable?

A rainy cold day is frustrating .... AND THEREFORE a rainy, cold day is unbearable.

Replace xyz with 'making a mistake', and the same logic will apply. It remains logically wrong to make the second LFT statement a conclusion that flows from the first.

LFT beliefs are not helpful

When you believe that the difficulties in your life are unbearable, your body functions differently as a result. LFT beliefs have consequences. They are not harmless or healthy. Believing that you can't stand something will cause you to feel emotions such as anxiety, depression, rage and shame. Your thoughts about your abilities will be negative and your problem-solving skills will be weakened. In a state of anxiety, caused by your LFT belief, you will not be functioning at your best. Your performance will be greatly affected.

LFT beliefs make you operate in a restricted way and cause unhealthy tension in your body. It's as if you are walking under a very low ceiling. The more you lower your tolerance, the more you lower this ceiling. The solution is, of course, to learn to deal with, and increase your tolerance to, difficulties.

Example

Let us return to the woman whose goal is to feel confident and speak eloquently in staff meetings. She feels anxious about remembering what she wants to say. She puts demands on herself to ensure that she remembers because going blank would be the end of the world. This demanding and catastrophizing belief causes her to feel anxious which then triggers her second belief about the state of her anxiety itself (that she must calm down). She catastrophizes the state of her anxiety and demands relaxation, causing further anxiety. Imagine that she also has an LFT belief about the state of her anxiety. She tells herself that she can't stand her feelings and that they are unbearable, as well as being horrible. This LFT belief is likely to further reinforce her demand to get rid of her anxiety, but it does the opposite. She is so intolerant of the sensations of anxiety that she feels them more, not less. This happens because she is now so sensitive to the emotion itself. Her mind is even more focused on her feelings and not on the meeting. She is now completely absorbed in her own world. Her low tolerance to anxiety is lowering the ceiling she is under. All she feels like doing is – you've guessed it – getting out of that meeting.

Her rigid intolerant belief is not helping her achieve her goal of confidence and eloquent speech. In fact, it will cause her throat to dry and her mind to focus on running away. As the body is now geared for the flight response, the energy used for recall is diverted to this function. Her body is reacting as if her colleagues are like a pride of lions looking at her and seeing lunch. If there was a pride of lions, i.e. she was actually under threat, then her body would gear into anxiety. It would divert the energy of many physical and mental functions to those that would be useful for running away. So in a state of anxiety she would not be geared up to presenting sales figures. Her rigid, catastrophizing, LFT beliefs would make her body and mind respond as if she was facing a pride of lions.

Self-acceptance vs self-damning

How you judge yourself when you do not get what you want is very important. This is about how you rate yourself when your desires are not met or when you fail to achieve your goals. How you rate yourself, or what you tell yourself and believe about yourself, makes a big difference to how you feel, think and behave. It greatly influences how well you perform and how happily and healthily you achieve your goals.

When you do not get what you want, you may judge that as failure; you have failed to get what you want. In reality, you may not always get things right – which is not the same as 'failing to' get things right. What you conclude about yourself as a result of this can be either healthy or unhealthy. A healthy conclusion would tend to be rational, realistic and logical. An unhealthy conclusion would be irrational, unrealistic and illogical.

When your belief about yourself is healthy and realistic it will help you to move forward, be problem-solving and constructive. It sets you up for achieving your goals. It also encourages you to get up and have another go or do things differently after disappointment or failure. It may cause you to feel upset or unhappy for a short period of time, because you have not been successful at getting what you want, but you learn from the experience and move on.

If your belief about yourself is unhealthy and unhelpful, it will cause you to put yourself down because you have not achieved what you wanted. In effect you turn the disappointment you experienced into an indication and proof of how bad, stupid or worthless you are. You believe things like 'I'm a failure because I failed', 'I'm worthless because I was rejected', 'I'm useless because I couldn't think of a solution' and so on. In CBT we call this a 'self-damning' belief. It means you rate yourself as a human being based on whether or not your demand was met.

Think back to the example of the child who plays the piano. She was already demanding that she must not make a mistake when she performs because doing so in front of everyone would be awful and unbearable. You already understand that such beliefs are unhealthy because they are rigid, unrealistic, illogical and unhelpful. They cause her anxiety and negative thinking. Now imagine that, as she sits down to do more practice, this belief is triggered because she is thinking about her performance. In her state of anxiety she will begin to focus on *how* she is playing all the time, instead of practising. This means she will disconnect from the music because she is operating in her own head and being hyper-vigilant. In this state the likelihood of making mistakes increases and she starts to notice that she is making mistakes. She then starts to believe that she is 'useless' because she keeps making mistakes. As this negative thought is entertained and repeated she starts to believe it and before long she is making herself more anxious because she now thinks a useless person like herself will be playing in front of the whole school. She then makes more demands to get things right and the unhealthy chain of her demand is now linked to the catastrophizing belief, LFT and self-damning belief.

Her overall belief now is:

- *I must not make a mistake when I play in front of the whole school and my friends. If I make a mistake:*
  - It would be the end of the world.
  - I would not cope.
  - It would prove that I'm useless.

It's easy to see how self-damning beliefs cause unhealthy negative emotions, thoughts and self-sabotaging behaviours.

Self-damning beliefs are rigid and inflexible

Self-damning beliefs are rigid and inflexible because they cause you to see yourself in one way and as a direct reflection of your negative goal or negative behaviour. No allowance is made for you to be anything else apart from 'useless', 'bad', 'worthless' or a 'failure'. You become your failure. You become your negative behaviour.

For example, if you hold the belief, 'I have to succeed because if I don't it proves that I'm a failure', you are not allowing or acknowledging the things that you are still succeeding at, for example breathing, washing, holding down a job, having friends and probably lots of other things as well. You are making a judgement about your entire self based on the one thing that you are focused on.

You can see how rigid and inflexible you can be about yourself when you criticize yourself in this way.

You may think, 'well, I am a failure because what I wanted was very important to me; it defined me'. I will respond by saying you are more than that important thing you defined yourself by. You are a million and one things. You are all of your biological and psychological traits and tendencies. You may be a brother, a sister, a father, an uncle, an aunt, a friend, a cook, and a football-loving, cricket-hating, barn-dancing person as well. You are more than just one thing that you define yourself by.

Rating yourself as totally bad or worthless is so rigid that it causes your body and your mind to feel the consequences of such a label or belief.

Self-damning is inconsistent with reality

It is not consistent with reality to believe that you are a total failure if you do not get what you are demanding. While you can show that you may have done badly, or that you may have failed at achieving what you were insisting on, you would not be able to prove that, as a result, you have now become a total failure as a human being. You can prove that you failed but not that you are a failure. You can prove that someone rejected you but not that you are now worthless as a person. When you believe you are a failure, by taking this to a logical conclusion you should be able to prove that from the moment you failed you continued to fail at everything else, including breathing.

For example, if you hold the belief, 'I must get my promotion because if I don't it would prove that I'm worthless' then you are effectively believing that you have no value at all. Everything about you becomes worthless from that moment on. You become a failure at everything in life.

Reality shows that you succeed at most things, and fail at some things. Reality shows that you are liked by many people, disliked by some and neither liked nor disliked by others. Reality shows that sometimes you make mistakes, other times you get things right. Reality shows that sometimes you perform brilliantly, sometimes badly, and at all of the standards in between. Reality shows that it is your performance and behaviour that vary, not your worth. But if you rate your worthiness by your performance then you will feel the consequences of it.

If you believe that, as a result of failing your examination you become a failure as a person, then why are you not failing at everything? If you become a failure because of something in particular then surely you become a failure at everything. So it is not true that you are a failure if you fail at one thing.

Again, you may say, 'but if I "feel" like a failure then surely I am one'. However, your feelings are not an indication of the truth. Your feelings are caused by how you are thinking. If your thinking is unhealthy, untrue or illogical then your feelings will be the result of such thinking.

Acknowledge that you are imperfect, because that is all your failures show and that you are human and fallible, like everyone else. Imagine that everything about you is represented by all the different fruits in a basket. The apple represents your failure at getting that promotion. Would you say that all the other fruit is ruined and should be thrown in the rubbish bin?

You may ask, 'if my worth is not dependent on my behaviour and performance or on anything at all, then what is it dependent on?' Your worth is not dependent on anything. You are a worthwhile but imperfect human being just because you breathe. I often explain this by asking that when you look at a new baby, do you question the worthiness of his or her life? Do you think that the loving parents look at their baby and think, 'he's worthwhile BUT he becomes a total failure if he is rejected by his first girlfriend, and he becomes unworthy if someone doesn't like him'? You wouldn't consider such thinking because you know it sounds so ridiculous and untrue. But you sometimes believe it about yourself.

What do you think about some of the truths you have believed until now?

Self-damning beliefs are not logical

It is not logical to conclude that you are a totally worthless person because you did not succeed or because you failed at something. This is an example of flawed common sense. It is a faulty leap of logic. If you fail the logical conclusion to make about yourself is that it proves you are not perfect, not that you are a total failure as a person.

Example

Consider the statement below. You can see that it is made up of two parts. Part one acknowledges that you failed at something. Let's call that something 'xyz'. The second statement is about the conclusion that follows from the first statement.

I failed at xyz .... AND THEREFORE I AM a failure as a person.

Replace xyz with 'getting things right' and the same logic will apply. It remains logically wrong to make the second statement.

I failed at getting things right ... AND THEREFORE I AM a failure as a person.

Self-damning beliefs are not helpful

It's easy to see that there are no benefits in rating yourself as 'worthless' or 'useless' or a 'failure' because of something – even a number of things – that have gone wrong in your life. When you make this huge leap from failing to achieve something (whether it is an exam, a promotion, a relationship – or even when you fail to remain calm and relaxed) to believing that you are a failure as a person, your body and mind will be affected by these beliefs.

Damning yourself in such a negative way is not only untrue and makes no sense at all, but it will have unfortunate consequences. This sort of belief causes a lot of harm. It makes you feel anxious and depressed, may cause you to feel irrationally angry with yourself and with other people and with life in general, and may also cause other unhealthy emotions.

I'm sure that there have been many times in your life when you have rated yourself in such a totally negative way. You may even hold such beliefs at the moment. You know what they cause you to feel and how they make you think. You also know that they cause this negative cycle of thinking, doing and believing as shown by the cycle diagram on page 31.

Self-damning beliefs limit your abilities and your potential. If, for example, you believe that you are 'useless' because of something that you can't do, or couldn't do last time you tried, like making a presentation, you know that by just thinking about standing up in public your negative self-doubting thoughts immediately creep into your mind and your heart starts to race.

The healthy way to handle this sort of situation is to:

- accept yourself as a worthwhile but fallible person; or

- you can also just rate your behaviour and performance and stop at that.

At this moment you may think 'it all sounds good but how?' The 'how' will come soon.

Example

Think back to the woman whose goal is to feel confident and to speak eloquently in staff meetings. She feels anxious about re-membering what she wants to say. She also has catastrophizing beliefs and LFT beliefs.

Imagine that she also has a self-damning belief linked to her demand about remembering, so she believes that her inability to remember is proof that she is a 'useless' person.

Now other thoughts about herself, not just about her abilities, start to invade her mind, causing further feelings of anxiety and tension in her body. Her body responds to the self-damning beliefs by causing her heart rate to go up and her muscles to tense. As she notices this anxiety, her second belief about anxiety also kicks in.

Now imagine that she goes on to damn herself more because she cannot control her feelings of anxiety. So being anxious is now further proof of how useless she is. This vicious cycle is preoc-cupying her mind and distancing her even further from being at the meeting. In such a state, her body and mind are definitely not set up for remembering what to say when her turn comes to speak. She feels like escaping from it all.

A quick recap

So far you have learned that unhealthy beliefs are at the heart of your unhealthy emotions and behaviours and that they influence your performance in a negative way too.

You have learned that unhealthy beliefs are rigid and inflexible, untrue, illogical and unhelpful.

You have learned that unhealthy beliefs are caused by taking what you want and turning it into an absolute MUST. So they come in the form of demands:

MUST
HAVE TO
GOT TO
ABSOLUTELY SHOULD
NEED TO

You have also learned that, flowing from such demands, you may then awfulize the badness of not getting what you are demanding. Awfulizing beliefs come in the form of:

TERRIBLE
AWFUL
HORRIBLE
END OF THE WORLD
CATASTROPHE

In that moment when your belief is triggered you believe that nothing worse can happen.

You've learned that you may also make difficulty unbearable. This is called low frustration tolerance. LFT beliefs come in the form of:

I CAN'T TOLERATE IT
I CAN'T COPE
I CAN'T STAND IT
IT'S UNBEARABLE

You have also learned that when your demand is not met you may totally damn yourself as a human being. You believe that you are a complete failure. Self-damning beliefs come in the form of:

I AM WORTHLESS
I AM STUPID
I AM USELESS
I AM A FAILURE
I AM BAD
I AM A LOSER

All unhealthy beliefs are rigid, untrue, illogical and unhelpful to you in terms of your goal achievement.

You have learned that all the above beliefs may be present in various combinations when the demand is triggered. Therefore an unhealthy belief might be:

- I must not make a mistake when I speak because if I do, it would be awful and unbearable and would prove that I'm a failure.

Unhealthy beliefs are based solely on your internal world view. They are based on your version of the truth as opposed to truth that is based on reality.

You have learned that unhealthy beliefs cause unhealthy negative emotions and self-sabotaging behaviours.

The concepts at the heart of healthy beliefs

If the unhealthy beliefs are rigid and inflexible, untrue, illogical and unhelpful, then your healthy beliefs will be flexible, true, logical and helpful to you.

Healthy beliefs are based on the union between your internal world view and external reality. That means your healthy beliefs are balanced.

Essentially healthy beliefs will help you focus and strive for goals and to plan for the worst, rather than avoid the possibility of having to face the worst.

Focus and strive for the best and plan for the worst.

Want to but I don't have to

Instead of the coercive 'MUST', a healthy belief is based on a WANT or desire coupled with an acceptance of what external reality can sometimes show us. The 'have to' is taken out of the equation.

Example

I want the day to be nice and sunny when I wake up but that does not mean that it has to be.

Or:

I'd like the day to be nice and sunny but I ACCEPT that there is a chance that it might not be.

So you focus on your desire but not in a coercive and demanding way.

Bad but not the end of the world

Instead of awfulizing the badness as if the world has ended, you accept that something bad has happened. However, as bad as it is, it is still not the end of the world. Once again this is a union between your internal view that something bad has happened and external reality, which shows that the world has not ended.

> ### Example
>
> It's bad that today is not nice and sunny but it's not the end of the world.
>
> Or:
>
> I don't like it that the day is not as I want but it's not awful.

Difficult but not unbearable

Instead of making difficulties unbearable, a healthy belief acknowledges your internal view that you are experiencing a difficulty. It also acknowledges that you are still alive and here to tell the tale.

> ### Example
>
> I find it difficult when the day is not nice and sunny but I can tolerate it.
>
> Or:
>
> I am worthy but I am fallible.

A healthy belief is based on accepting yourself unconditionally. This means you do not rate yourself at all; you rate your behaviour and your performance. As a human being you are made up of positive, negative and neutral qualities. A negative quality does not negate the rest of your worthiness, so a healthy belief acknowledges that you do sometimes make mistakes because you are fallible. It does not say that you are a mistake – in fact, it acknowledges the whole you as neither good nor bad, but as someone who sometimes does good and sometimes does bad. It acknowledges that you are a worthy but imperfect human being.

Example

If I make a mistake it doesn't mean I am a failure. I am fallible but remain worthwhile. My worth does not depend on whether I make a mistake or not.

In the next chapter you will learn more about how healthy beliefs are true, logical and helpful to you.

Exercise

What would it mean to you if you believed that you are a worthwhile human being regardless of whether or not you achieve something?

How would an attitude of 'I want to but I don't have to' affect how you feel and how you go about doing things?

What do you think you would be able to achieve if you did not catastrophize failing?

CHAPTER 3

Your goals

This chapter is about setting personally motivating goals after a period of self-reflection. You will learn how to use words that create vivid, emotive pictures in your mind of what you want to achieve.

Reflect on what you want

This is vital for goal achievement. In order to clarify what we want we need to assess worthwhile needs and wants.

SMART goals:

- Specific
- Measurable
- Achievable
- Realistic
- Time-oriented

Using the **SMART** model will help you learn how to set goals appropriately.

Current goal-sabotaging beliefs

Learn how to identify which of your current thoughts and beliefs are stopping you from achieving your goals.

Goal-achievement beliefs to support your SMART goal

You will be guided towards understanding and constructing the healthy counterparts to your negative beliefs.

Personally persuasive reasons

This section is about identifying and writing down all the benefits and advantages of having healthy beliefs and the disadvantages of maintaining unhealthy beliefs.

By writing a list of persuasive and positive points you will be creating an invaluable tool to help you in the process of attaining your goals. You can also write down the consequences of your negative thoughts and beliefs. This will remind you of why you are putting in the effort to make a change.

Reflect on what you want

- Your balance wheel
- Goal-sabotaging beliefs
- Goal-achievement beliefs

Here you will learn how to scan your life for the areas that you wish to improve so that you can figure out what is stopping you from moving forward.

You have already started this process by thinking and reflecting. So far, you have been introduced to the concept of emotional responsibility, which is about understanding that you are generally accountable for how you feel, think, and go about doing things. It is not the past that is causing your feelings but what you believe about yourself, or ways you have been conditioned into thinking about yourself, other people and about life. Once you have accepted this important insight of emotional responsibility and accountability, what you can achieve becomes more realistic.

If the suggestion that you are responsible for how you feel and what you want feels daunting, make a note of your feelings for the time being and carry on reading. If, however, it feels like a window opening, you may be getting a sense of possible freedom and excitement. Knowing that you are responsible for your feelings and for your life means that there is a way to make changes, to start thinking about how you want your life to be and what you want to achieve. Emotional responsibility is about tapping into your potential with the knowledge that what you wish to change is possible. You may be allowing yourself to dream about how you want your future to be.

You have perhaps begun to understand that your beliefs are at the heart of your emotions, thoughts and behaviour. Remember that beliefs are judgemental or evaluative thoughts. Your beliefs, thoughts, emotions and behaviours all influence and feed off each other so you condition yourself and reinforce what you think about yourself and your abilities.

You can now see that it is having unhealthy beliefs that stops you from moving forward and causes feelings like anxiety, depression, guilt and hurt. These unhealthy beliefs make you feel that you are bad, useless or a failure. It isn't you that's at fault, but your beliefs about yourself. You have now understood that these unhealthy beliefs are not true or consistent with reality; they tend be rigid and inflexible. You have understood that they do not make any sense and they do not help you.

You know that there is a different, healthy way of thinking – a healthy version of your unhealthy beliefs. The healthy beliefs are flexible, true and consistent with reality, they make sense and they are helpful to you.

Beliefs are like a pair of glasses you wear in certain situations. In some instances, you may wear the 'wrong' glasses that make the world seem unfocused. In others, you may wear glasses that help you see clearly and in colour. Getting a new prescription for the right kind of glasses is like changing the old unhealthy beliefs and investing in your new healthy beliefs.

You can see that it is possible to change your beliefs, which will give you healthier emotions and help you to think constructive and positive thoughts. Now you may start reflecting on what you want to achieve or how you want your life to be.

The first thing is to scan your life and the things that are important to you. You can do this by creating your own balance wheel to reflect all the key things in your life in a broad and general way. You do not need to be specific at this stage. It is about looking at the overall big picture.

Your balance wheel

The circle below represents some of the significant areas in your life. It is by no means an exhaustive list. For example, you may wish to include a section for retirement instead of career or education and add a spiritual or political section. This circle can include any areas you like. You may already know what your goals are but you may want to think about other areas too.

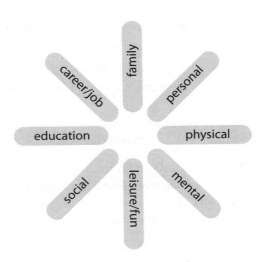

Family

This section is all about your family life and your relationships with parents, siblings, children or other relatives.

Family life can be a source of great happiness or it can be full of emotional, behavioural and communication problems. If your family life is important to you it is worth reflecting on this area. Problems in families may be due to past unresolved issues, or difficulties in forgiving someone's behaviour. There may be present difficulties such as financial stress which impacts on communication and mood, and worries about the future, such as fears about children leaving home and the consequences of that on your relationship.

Family issues may also be about closeness and a feeling that you could be closer. They may be about your relationship with your parents or a recognition that you may want to do more, for example visiting more often and the emotional consequences of that.

If this is an area in your life that you would like to improve, rate your level of contentment between 0 and 10. Zero represents the worst in terms of happiness and 10 represents complete contentment about your family life. If there is no room for improvement at present, it is not a priority for you.

Example

James is having a difficult relationship with his father. In public his father appears to be more proud of his older brother, Mark. James is angry and hurt about this, and also feels guilty about his emotions because he is close to his brother.

James' feelings have started to affect his relationship with his father. He has started to talk in a sarcastic manner whenever his father speaks. James' father doesn't understand why his son is acting in this way and when he confronts him there is only silence and sulks. As a consequence James has started to visit his family a lot less than he used to.

He rates his family relationships as being at 4 out of 10 and wants them to be at 7 or 8.

Personal

This area is about your personal life. It may be about your relationships, or any other personal difficulties you may have, for example, shyness or feelings of anxiety when you are socializing. It may be about worrying about rejection when you go on a date or it may be about stopping smoking.

It could also be about your personal development. Personal development may involve learning about yourself, making peace with the past and moving on, understanding yourself, or gaining insight and learning about your psychological health. This book may already have started the process for you.

Where would you rank your level of satisfaction with your personal life (0 = zero satisfaction and 10 = totally satisfied)? How important is this to you in your overall big picture?

Physical

This is about assessing how satisfied you are with your physical health or your body shape and weight. Your physical health may be one of the areas you wish to change. You may wish to exercise more or lose weight. You may have dreams about running a marathon. This may be the time to start thinking and implementing your ideas.

Where would you rank your level of satisfaction with your physical life (0 = zero satisfaction and 10 = totally satisfied)? How important is this to you in your overall big picture?

Mental

The area of mental health is one where many people now seek professional help. Knowing when you need help and looking for it is in itself an excellent goal. Do you tend to suffer from depression or anxiety to such an extent that it often interrupts your life? Maybe you are suffering from problems like self loathing, panic disorder or obsessive compulsive disorder. Mental health problems are common and speaking to your GP first is highly recommended.

Mental health is also about how you feel generally. For example, you may wish to be calmer and more positive in your thinking. Maybe you have always wanted to see the glass half full but cannot quite manage it.

Maybe you have tried to be positive but weren't quite able to stay that way and want to know why?

Scan this area of your overall big picture and rate your level of satisfaction on a scale of 0 to 10 (0 = not satisfied at all and 10 = totally satisfied). How significant is this for you?

Leisure/fun

You may feel that you have fun in your life but how much time do you set aside to leisure activities and doing things that are fun just for you? You may have devoted more time to having fun when you were younger but work, family or financial commitments may have meant that it became less of a priority over time. You may want to commit more time to this area of your life because all work and no play is not as fulfilling as it used to be.

It is not uncommon to be doing well and striving for the things that you want, but noticing that perhaps you are not smiling as much as you used to. Maybe most of your friends are now married and the things they want to do have changed. You may still want to be out there partying and dancing, but you are at a loss as to how to start up again.

Reflect on this part of your life and rate your level of satisfaction between 0 and 10 (0 = totally unsatisfied and 10 = totally satisfied). How significant is this area in your overall big picture?

Social

How is your social life and how satisfied are you with it? You may have been focused on your career, on your family life or even on your education in such an intense way that this area of your life has been neglected. If you know you have made this a conscious choice and feel happy with reducing the priority of your social life that's fine, but do you find yourself working late and not having time to return your friends' calls? Have they stopped calling because you are always too busy to accept social invitations? Do you feel that you are neglecting this part of your life and that you are unhappy about it? Maybe you have moved jobs and find yourself away from most of your friends and the idea of making new friends feels like too much hard work?

Think about your social life and rate your level of satisfaction on a scale of 0 to 10 (0 = totally poor and 10 = totally fantastic). How important is your social life in the overall scheme of your life?

Education

You may have started work quite young and now that you are more settled you are thinking about returning to education. It could be that you want to continue with your higher education in order to get a more satisfying career. Whatever your reason, you have started to think about it. Perhaps you are surprised at yourself because you are thinking about studying and education as being fun. At this stage do not allow your feelings to stop your thoughts. You are not committing to anything. Just reflect on this area and assess whether you feel it has become important to you.

Rate your level of satisfaction on a scale of 0 to 10 (0 = totally unsatisfied, 10 = totally satisfied). How important is this part of your life to you now when you consider your big picture?

Career/job

You often hear that most people are not totally happy with their careers, and that many people are opting for self-employment or changing their jobs. Are you feeling dissatisfied with your job, especially if you spend at least seven hours a day doing it?

How do you feel about your work? What do you think about your career? Is this what you imagined yourself doing when you were younger? Are you unsure about what you want to do but you know that this is not it?

Think about this area in your life and rate your level of satisfaction on a scale of 0 to 10 (0 = totally dissatisfied and 10 = totally satisfied). How important is this part of your life in comparison to others at this stage in your life?

Importance of what you want

It's easy to see how important it is to reflect on all of this as part of your overall scheme of things. It is almost impossible to achieve goals if they are not important or if you do not get some personal benefit from them. The previous section helped you to scan your life and reflect on your current position, i.e. where you are now. It was about being honest with yourself about your current level of satisfaction and thinking about how badly you want to change it.

You can be dissatisfied with one area of your life but tolerate it because your focus is on another part that you feel is more important at the moment. Your goal is your vision of the future that you want. It is a vision that you care about. It should invoke an emotion when you think about it; either a positive one, indicating that you have a healthy positive attitude about it or a negative one because you have unhealthy beliefs about yourself. Remember that ABC model?

A stands for the trigger or event

B stands for beliefs – either healthy or unhealthy

C stands for consequence – emotions, thoughts, behaviours and symptoms

Achieving or not achieving your goal would be the trigger, or A.

Your belief about yourself, or your skills when you think about your goal, or the problem you are having with it is B.

Your feelings, thoughts and what you see yourself doing is C.

If your belief (B) about yourself, others or the world when you think about your goal (A) is healthy, then your emotions (C) will be positive and constructive, but if your belief is unhealthy then your feelings will be destructive.

If you say that you want something but do not feel anything about it when you imagine it, then perhaps you need time to reflect on how important it is for you at this stage in your life.

Example

Phil has been married for three years and has a one-year-old daughter. He has a happy marriage and is enjoying his new family. His family is the most important part of his life and his personal life comes a close second. He is content with both of these areas. However, he has been neglecting his physical health and, apart from walking to the tube station everyday on his way to work, he does no exercise. Since the birth of his daughter his physical health has become important to him. He also feels that leisure activities and his social life have taken a dive and he wants to inject more energy into them. His job is not very good but it pays the mortgage. He does not want to look for another because it is 9–5, which means he can be at home with his family without feeling stressed or having to work long hours.

Once he reflected on them, his feelings about the different areas of his life were as follows:

Rate of satisfaction

Marks out of 10		Priority
Family	8	1
Personal	8	2
Physical	5	3
Mental	7	6
Leisure	6	4
Social	4	5
Education	6	7
Career	3	8

Phil may wish to make a small improvement in his family and personal life to raise their ranking from 8 to 9, or he may choose to leave them as they are because he is very satisfied with them. The areas of his life that may need attention are his physical health first, followed by leisure and social activities.

Look at the areas of your life that you are currently dissatisfied with or the areas that you want to improve. Begin to prioritize them in order of importance so number 1 is the most important area in your life and so on.

Exercise

Go back to your balance wheel and think about the different areas of your life. Rate your level of satisfaction for each and then prioritize your list.

Setting SMART goals

Goals reflect the way you want things to be. They are your desires, the things that you want to happen, the dreams you wish to fulfil. You are constantly setting goals and keeping an eye on the things that are going to happen in the future, like birthdays, anniversaries or other important events. Human beings are naturally goal-oriented.

You set goals from the moment you wake up, such as for going to work and getting there on time. You may have lunchtime goals, social goals, supermarket and clothes shopping goals. All of these activities are about visualizing something in the future, then moving towards it, and making it happen. Having the ability to focus, imagine and visualize the goal in a vivid way helps you move forward.

The more significant your goal, the stronger is its pulling power. So how do you make your goal vivid and colourful so that you can imagine it? Think about something that you have looked forward to in the past, for example, planning a party or going on holiday. You start thinking about a holiday, then you work out where and when and how much you want to spend. Do you want to go in July, August or September? You start looking through brochures or searching on the internet.

By the time you have completed your plans, your holiday goal has become **SMART**: Specific, Measurable, Achievable, Realistic, Time-oriented. Now you can visualize it and imagine yourself relaxing by the pool or skiing down snowy slopes, having drinks after sunset or enjoying a nice meal. You may be planning how one day you will go to the beach and the day after on an excursion. You are now focused on your goal. What's the likelihood that after a week or so of this focused thinking you will be booking your holiday?

SMART goals help you visualize the end result more clearly and vividly.

Specific

Specific means that your goal is clear, so it is about the where, how, and what. A specific goal gives you a clear picture of the outcome. Simply wanting a salary increase is not specific, it is only specific if you talk about how much of an increase you are looking for. Wanting to get fit is not specific. It does not create a picture of what 'fit' means and neither does 'I want to lose weight'. It is about how much weight you want to lose. You may be thinking 'I want to feel happier'. Once again, this is vague and does not create a picture of what being 'happier' means.

You may be considering getting another job. If you are not careful that's all you'll get – just another job. It is important to be specific about the type of job you want and the things you want to be doing in that new role.

The more you concentrate on making your goal specific, the better you will visualize it and strive towards it. Remember that you are naturally goal directed.

Measurable

Goals need to be measurable so that you can assess how well you have done and what you still need to do to improve on your result. It is important that your goals are clear and tangible as this means that there will be proof that you are achieving – or not achieving – your goal in some way. For example, if you plan to lose weight and have the specific goal of wanting to lose one stone, you can check that you are moving towards your goal by weighing yourself. You will have evidence to measure.

Achievable

Your goal needs to be achievable rather than based on wishful thinking. For example, you may hope to win the lottery and you think that by carrying out some ritual it becomes achievable. You may say, 'what if that was possible?' Just look at the results. Is this what reality shows you? Millions of people spend time doing the lottery but most will not be successful.

Achievable goals have to be attainable and feasible. How feasible is what you want? For example, swimming the Atlantic Ocean solo, non-stop would be in the category of unachievable.

Realistic

Realistic goals are sensible. They tend to be based on fact and the reality of life. This doesn't mean that you should downgrade your desires but ask yourself if they are possible. Unrealistic goals, ideas and expectations tend to have the words *always*, *never*, or *all the time* in them. They are irrational. For example, wanting never to feel anxious again is just not realistic. Always wanting to be happy or wanting everyone to like you are two common examples of irrational goals, as is wanting to *always* have the feeling of being in love, despite 20 years of marriage.

Time-oriented

This is about how long you think it will take you to reach your goal. It is good to focus on time because this provides the energy and motivation you need to be healthy and realistic about what you want to achieve. You may start putting unreasonable pressure on yourself to achieve something instead of reviewing your time frame. Without a time element, you might lose focus and allow yourself to drift away from what you want. Focusing on time indicates that you are ready to commit to it.

Achieving your goals depends on whether you have healthy beliefs about yourself and your skills – which will help you achieve them – or unhealthy beliefs that will stop you from moving towards them positively.

When you put all the **SMART** elements together you start to create a vivid, 'all singing, all dancing' goal. If your goal fails on any of the **SMART** categories then it is no longer **SMART** and you need to go back and modify it.

A **SMART** goal sets you up for success and your healthy beliefs provide the energy and drive for you to move towards it.

Example

Remember Phil in the last example? He reflected on the different areas in his life and identified that he needed to concentrate on his physical health. He now wants to lose one stone in weight.

Losing a stone in weight is his priority goal.

Losing one stone in weight is not a **SMART** goal because it does not fulfil all the criteria. So Phil needs to ask himself the following questions:

- Is my goal of wanting to lose one stone specific?
- Is it measurable?
- Is it achievable?
- Is it realistic?
- Is it time-oriented?

The goal is specific in that Phil is clear about how much weight he wants to lose. It is also measurable. It is achievable. It may be realistic.

However, the time element is missing, making it difficult to know whether or not it is realistic. If the time element is one week, it becomes unrealistic. The fact that the time element is missing may indicate that Phil is not ready or fully committed to his goal, so he may not be motivated enough to implement it.

Exercise

Look back to the last exercise where you rated your level of satisfaction in the different areas of your life and prioritized them in the context of your bigger picture. Choose one significant area that you are unsatisfied with.

Reflect on this important area and think about how you want it to be for you.

Write down your **SMART** goal about your significant choice. Ensure it meets all the **SMART** criteria.

Current goal-sabotaging beliefs

When you set a goal that means something to you, a number of things can happen.

- You may start to create pictures and images in your head.
- You may start having an internal dialogue about yourself or your abilities.
- You may start to have feelings or emotions.
- You may start doing something or feeling like you want to do something.
- You may start to get physiological sensations in your body.
- You may experience all or any combination of these things.

This section is about experiencing unhealthy emotions that stop you from planning and putting your goal-directed solutions into action. If you want to achieve something but find you are not succeeding, something is stopping you. The easiest way to gain insight into this blockage is to check your emotions and thoughts when you imagine your goal.

Think back to what you learned about your different emotions, the healthy negative ones and the unhealthy negative ones. In the CBT model, unhealthy emotions are caused by unhealthy beliefs that are rigid and inflexible, inconsistent with reality, illogical and unhelpful to you in terms of your goal achievement. Now you will learn to identify your current, unhealthy, goal-sabotaging beliefs by becoming aware of your unhealthy emotions and thoughts.

When you imagine something, or think about what you want to do, you may experience different emotions. This can be quite confusing. For example, thinking about your goal might trigger feelings of anxiety (un-healthy) about whether you will succeed, or guilt about taking time away from your family (unhealthy), or concern (healthy) about the work that it may involve.

Taking a systematic, sensible approach is one of the best ways of under-standing these varied emotions. This is all with the aim of identifying your goal-sabotaging beliefs at this point. Later on, you will learn how to change them in order to free yourself from their grip.

Using the ABC framework to keep the model in mind will help you identify your various emotions and thoughts.

Example

Jane is a 35-year-old married woman with two children. Her husband is a self-employed electrician and she works in the Human Resources department of a corporate company. An op-portunity has arisen to do a part-time diploma course in psy-chology, which her company will fund, and it's a subject she's always been interested in. The application form has a due date three months from now. Jane has been avoiding filling in the application form, as she is in a dilemma as to whether she should apply. She wants to do it but her feelings and thoughts are nega-tive. She is wondering whether she could manage it and is scared about the potential hard work. She is also anxious about how she would feel if the work meant that she would be spending a few nights a week studying, instead of being with her children and husband.

Jane's goal

In this example, you can see that Jane has a goal – to apply for a diploma in psychology – but when she thinks about it she feels anxious.

This is a **SMART** goal because it is specific in that Jane knows what course she wants to do. It is not vague. It is measurable in that she has an application form to complete. It is achievable by filling in the application form. It is realistic, tangible and time-oriented – she needs to send in her application before the due date in three months' time.

Jane's emotions and thoughts

Jane has a number of emotions that are stopping her from completing and sending the application form. The most dominant emotion is fear. You can assume that her fear-based emotion is anxiety rather than concern because her thoughts are negative and her behaviour is avoidant.

She is anxious about whether she can succeed in getting the psychology diploma because it could be very hard. She has an anxiety about how she would feel if she had to spend time away from her family. It is very likely that she may also be anxious about feeling guilt although the guilt state will probably be triggered later on.

This may become an issue after she starts her course if she does not anticipate it and move on from it now. She can still change this emotional state even after she starts the diploma.

Jane's ABC

In Jane's case, the 'A' in the ABC – the event or trigger – is applying for the diploma in psychology. Her goal triggers her feelings of anxiety.

Her feelings of anxiety are the emotional consequences. These are the 'C' in the ABC.

A	B	C
I'm thinking about applying for a diploma in psychology and it might be hard	➡ B	➡ Anxiety
How will I feel if it means time away from my family?	➡ B	➡ Guilt

Since Jane has two states of anxiety, she will have two unhealthy anxiety-causing beliefs – one per state. She is also likely to have a belief that would cause guilt. So she should be working to change three unhealthy beliefs in this example.

All that can be said about 'B' at this stage is that Jane has unhealthy beliefs because she has feelings of anxiety and possibly guilt.

Example

Simon is a 40-year-old single man who works as a teacher. Ten years ago he discovered meditation and spirituality and started putting both into practice for personal development reasons. His work has become increasingly more demanding, which has led him to give up his meditation in the last six months. He has started to feel low because he is finding it more and more difficult to feel the desire to get up earlier so that he can practise his meditation. Every night he sets his alarm for 6 a.m. but when it rings, he switches it off and sleeps until 7 a.m. He feels confused by this change and has become angry, doubtful, negative and cynical about his spirituality. He says that he started practising meditation because he thought it would have sorted him out by now but it hasn't.

Simon's goal

Simon's goal is to connect with himself and not feel low.

This is not a **SMART** goal at the moment. It is not specific — it is vague. It is partly measurable in that he can check if he is no longer feeling low but it is not complete because he has not described what signs he would be looking out for to help him understand that he has connected with himself. It is achievable in that he can move on from his low feelings but it is unclear what connecting with himself means, so there is a question mark about whether it is achievable. The same applies to whether or not his goal is realistic: it does not have a time frame.

Simon needs to reflect more on what he wants to achieve so he can have a better idea of how he wants to feel, think and be.

You can see that the goal is not clearly defined. It is difficult to get a clear image of Simon's goal without making an assumption.

On further reflection, Simon understands that what he wants is to be able to get up at 6 a.m. so he can meditate. He also wants to *feel* a desire to get up at 6 a.m. He wants to have positive thoughts about meditation and his spirituality as he used to. He wants to make this change by working through these issues over the next two months. This is now a **SMART** goal. Can you see why it is **SMART**?

Simon's emotions and thoughts

Simon's dominant emotion is depression. Depression is caused by unhealthy beliefs about failure or loss. He is feeling low because he is failing to get up at 6 a.m. to practise his meditation despite setting his alarm clock. It is not a feeling of sadness because he is stuck and is now having negative and cynical thoughts. He is not feeling a positive emotion when his alarm clock goes off. He is also feeling unhealthy anger with spirituality because he thought that it would have protected him from getting into this emotional state. He has not managed to rid himself of this feeling, so he is stuck.

Simon's ABC

Simon's problem started when he could not succeed at being able to meditate regularly. This is his trigger or 'A' in the ABC. He felt depressed about this failure and his feelings of depression are 'C' in the ABC. He also noticed that he did not have positive feelings when he wanted to practise his meditation, another trigger or 'A' that he felt even more depressed about. He also felt angry when he thought about his spirituality. Thinking about his spirituality was another trigger or 'A', and his feelings of anger are 'C' in the ABC.

A	B	C
I'm not managing to get up at 6 am as planned to practise my meditation	➡ B	➡ Depression
I don't feel like meditating	➡ B	➡ Depression
Spirituality didn't sort me out	➡ B	➡ Anger

At this stage you would not know what the beliefs ('B') are in the above three ABCs. All that you can say is that they are unhealthy because they are causing Simon's unhealthy feelings of depression and anger. His feelings are unhealthy because he is not managing to fulfil his goal and his thoughts are now both negative and cynical. His behaviour is unhealthy because it is not helping him fulfil his goal.

Exercise – Step 1

Start by writing down your **SMART** goal on a piece of paper as 'A' in the ABC model. Imagine yourself with your goal achieved. Now ask yourself: what are you experiencing emotionally? What emotions are stopping you from achieving it?

Go back to Chapter 1 and use the tables about emotions to write down your own feelings.

Step 2

Start with writing down your **SMART** goal.

Example: I want to lose 1 stone in weight in 2 months by eating healthily and exercising 3 times a week.

What are you experiencing emotionally when you think about your goal? (You may write 'stressed', 'upset' or other expressions of emotion.)

Example: Scared that I might not lose 1 stone, stressed at the thought of exercising 3 times a week, down about not eating what I want when I want.

Write down the negative unhealthy emotions that are blocking you from achieving your goal. (Go back to Chapter 1 and use the tables about emotions to help you.)

Example: Anxiety about not managing to lose 1 stone in 2 months.

Anxiety about exercising 3 times a week.

Depressed at the thought of not eating what I want when I want.

Now construct your 'A' and 'C' in the ABC ('A' is the trigger of the emotion, 'B' is the unknown belief, 'C' is the emotion). Triggers can be thoughts, sensations or events about the past, present or future. They can also be images and pictures.

Example:

A	B	C
I might not lose 1 stone in 2 months	➡ Belief	➡ Anxiety
Exercising 3 times a week	➡ Belief	➡ Anxiety
Can't eat what I want and when I want	➡ Belief	➡ Depressed

Identifying your current sabotaging beliefs

Earlier you learned how to do an overall scan of the various areas in your life and assess your level of satisfaction for each. As a result of this you may have started thinking about how you want these areas to be for you in the future, i.e. what goals you have in mind for them. You then learned to write goals in a **SMART** way to enable you to have a vivid picture of your goal and to trigger the emotional states that are blocking you. It is your emotions that will help you identify your unhealthy, goal-sabotaging beliefs. Your unhealthy beliefs, which may be stored deep in your subconscious mind, cause your emotions, negative thoughts, and unhelpful behaviours. It is easy to use your emotions as the hook to fish out your unhealthy beliefs.

You will remember that unhealthy beliefs are rigid and inflexible, inconsistent with reality, illogical and unhelpful. You learned that there are four types of unhealthy beliefs: 'demand', 'must' or 'have to'; the

catastrophizing beliefs; the low frustration tolerance beliefs; and the self-
or other- or world-damning ones. This section will help you to identify
the unhealthy belief that causes each of your unhealthy negative
emotions.

So far you have identified 'A' and 'C' in the ABC model. You may or may
not have all four unhealthy beliefs but you should be looking out for at
least two for each emotion. Usually the 'demand' type and one or more
of the other three are likely to be present.

The easiest way to identify these beliefs is by imagining or thinking about
the trigger, focusing on the emotion you feel, asking yourself a number
of questions and writing down the answer for each question.

What type of questions do you ask?

1. To identify the demand belief you ask:
   What do my feelings tell me about what I'm demanding/insisting
   on when I'm thinking about xyz? What am I saying MUST or
   MUST NOT happen?

2. To identify the catastrophizing belief you ask:
   What do my feelings tell me about how bad it will be if I fail at
   getting what I'm demanding when I think about xyz? Are they telling
   me it will be bad, awful, terrible, horrible, the end of the world?

3. To identify the low frustration tolerance belief you ask:
   What do my feelings tell me about how difficult it will be if I fail to
   get what I'm demanding when I think about xyz? Are they telling
   me it will be difficult (hard, tough, frustrating) or unbearable (can't
   cope, can't stand it, can't tolerate it)?

4. To identify the self-damning, other-damning or world-damning
   belief you ask:

What do my feelings tell me about what I think of myself if I fail to get what I'm demanding when I think about xyz? Are they telling me that I failed – full stop – or are they telling me that I'm a failure (unworthy, useless, loser, rubbish, bad, weak)?

Jane's ABC in the previous example:

Jane's goal was to apply for a diploma in psychology in three months' time.

A	B	C
I'm thinking about applying for a diploma in psychology and it might be hard	➡ B	➡ Anxiety
How will it feel if it means time away from my family?	➡ B	➡ Anxiety
And if she did do the course and found out she was taking time away from her family		
I'm doing the course and spending too much time away	➡ B	➡ Guilt

Since Jane has two states of anxiety, she will have two unhealthy anxiety-causing beliefs respectively. She is also likely to have a belief that would cause guilt.

The xyz in the questions relates to the statements under the 'A' in Jane's example.

Jane identifies the 'B' in the first ABC

Jane thinks about applying for the diploma course, which might turn out to be very hard. She focuses on her feeling of anxiety. She then asks:

What do my feelings tell me about what I'm demanding/insisting on when I'm thinking about the diploma and how hard it might be? What am I saying MUST or MUST NOT happen?

Jane identifies that she is demanding that she MUST find it easy. She then asks:

What do my feelings tell me about how bad it will be if I do not find it easy when I think the diploma MUST be easy? Are they telling me it will be bad or awful, terrible, horrible, the end of the world?

Jane identifies that it would be bad but not terrible. She then asks herself:

What do my feelings tell me about how difficult it will be if I do not find the course easy when I think it MUST be easy? Are they telling me it will be difficult (hard, tough, frustrating) or unbearable (can't cope, can't stand it)?

Jane identifies that she believes she will not be able to cope if she finds it difficult. She then asks herself:

What do my feelings tell me about what I think of myself if I find it difficult when I think that it MUST be easy? Are they telling me that I failed at finding it easy full stop or are they telling me that I'm a failure (unworthy, useless, loser, bad, weak) because I might find it difficult?

Jane identifies that she believes it would mean that she is stupid.

So Jane's anxiety-causing belief – when she thinks about applying for the diploma which might turn out to be hard – is:

I MUST find the diploma easy and not hard. If I find it hard then I won't cope and it would prove that I'm stupid.

Putting it in the ABC model, Jane's first ABC is as follows:

A	B	C
I'm thinking about applying for a diploma in psychology and it might be hard ➡	I must find the diploma easy. If I find it hard then I won't cope and it will prove that I'm stupid	➡ Anxiety

Jane identifies the 'B' in the second ABC

Jane allows herself to explore her thoughts about what she would feel if the course meant that she might need to take time away from her family. She focuses on her feeling of anxiety about this. She then asks herself:

What do my feelings of anxiety tell me about what I'm demanding/insisting on when I'm wondering how I will feel if the diploma might mean taking time away from my family? What am I saying MUST or MUST not happen?

Jane identifies that she is saying that she MUST know how she will feel if she will need to take time away from her family. She then asks herself:

What do my feelings tell me about how bad it is that I don't know for certain how I will feel if I'm going to take time away from my family when I'm thinking that I MUST know? Are my feelings of anxiety telling me it is bad or that it is awful?

Jane concludes that her feelings are telling her it is awful she doesn't know for certain how she will feel if she needs to take time away from her family. She then asks herself:

What do my feelings tell me about how difficult it is for me to not know for certain how I will feel if I will need to take time away from my family, when I'm saying that I MUST know? Are they telling me it is difficult for me or are they telling me I can't stand it?

Jane concludes that her feelings are telling her she cannot stand not knowing how she will feel if she will need to take time away from her family. She then asks herself:

What do my feelings tell me about what I think about myself when I do not know how I will feel if I will need to take time away from my family, when I'm saying that I MUST know? Are they telling me that I just won't know at the moment or are they telling me that I'm a failure because I don't know?

Jane concludes that she is putting herself down for not knowing for certain if she will need to spend time away from her family if she starts the course.

So Jane's second anxiety-causing belief when she is wondering how she will feel if she needs to take time away from her family is:

I MUST know how I will feel if I need to take time away from my family when I'm doing the course. It's awful that I don't know and I cannot stand not knowing how I will feel.

Jane's second ABC looks as follows:

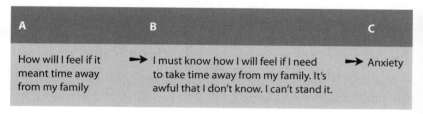

A	B	C
How will I feel if it meant time away from my family	I must know how I will feel if I need to take time away from my family. It's awful that I don't know. I can't stand it.	Anxiety

Jane identifies the 'B' in the third ABC

Jane begins to reflect on how she would feel if she did start the course and had to spend time away from her family during the week because of her study. She identifies that she would feel the emotion of guilt. She then asks herself:

What do my feelings of guilt tell me about what I'm demanding/insisting on when I'm imagining myself spending time away from my family to study for my diploma? What am I saying MUST or MUST not happen?

Jane identifies that she is saying that she MUST not take time away from her family during the week because this would be more time apart from them on top of her daytime work. She then asks herself:

What do my feelings tell me about how bad it would be if I took more time away from my family for the diploma when I'm saying that I MUST not do this? Are my feelings telling me it is bad or awful?

She concludes that she is telling herself that it would be awful if she did that. She then asks:

What do my feelings tell me about how hard it would be to take time away from my family when I'm telling myself that I MUST not do that? Are my feelings telling me it would difficult or unbearable for me?

Jane believes that she thinks she would find it hard but not unbearable. Finally, she asks herself:

What do my feelings tell me about what I would think of myself if I took time away from my family when I'm saying that I MUST NOT do that? Are they telling me that I won't fail at being a good mother even though I would take time away from my family or are they telling that taking time away from my family would mean I'm a bad mother and wife?

Jane concludes that she would indeed be putting herself down and telling herself that she is a bad mother and wife.

So, Jane's full unhealthy guilt-causing belief would be:

I MUST not take time away from my family during the week to work on my diploma. Doing that would be awful and it would prove I'm a bad mother and wife.

Putting it in the ABC model, Jane's third ABC is as follows:

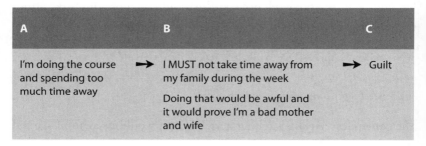

A	B	C
I'm doing the course and spending too much time away	I MUST not take time away from my family during the week Doing that would be awful and it would prove I'm a bad mother and wife	Guilt

Exercise

Write down the ABCs you worked on from the last exercise.

Take one ABC at a time and ask yourself similar questions, using the following template as a guide:

Q1: What do my feelings tell me about what I'm demanding/ insisting on when I'm thinking about xyz? What am I saying MUST or MUST not happen?

Q2: What do my feelings tell me about how bad it will be if I fail at getting what I'm demanding when I think about xyz? Are they telling me it will be bad, or awful, horrible, the end of the world?

Q3: What do my feelings tell me about how difficult it will be if I fail at getting what I'm demanding when I think about xyz? Are they telling me it will be difficult (hard, tough, frustrating) or unbearable (can't cope, can't stand it, can't tolerate it)?

Q4: What do my feelings tell me about what I think of myself if I fail at getting what I'm demanding when I think about xyz? Are they telling me that I failed full stop or are they telling me that I'm a failure (unworthy, useless, loser, rubbish, bad, weak etc.)?

Write down the full unhealthy belief for each of your ABCs. Remember all or some of the four unhealthy beliefs may be present in each of your ABCs. Refer to Jane's examples for guidance.

Put all the unhealthy beliefs under the ABC framework.

Goal achievement beliefs to support your SMART goal

Beliefs that set you up for goal achievement are the healthy versions of the unhealthy sabotaging beliefs. You will recall that healthy beliefs are flexible, consistent with reality, logical and helpful to you.

Healthy beliefs are based on what you want to achieve (internal reality) alongside the acceptance of external reality in order to make it balanced, powerful, logical and helpful. So your healthy beliefs take the laws of reality into account while focusing on what is important to you. This means:

Hoping, wanting and striving for the best but accepting and planning for the worst-case scenario by negating the demand.

Accepting that bad things happen with the knowledge that this won't be the worst thing that could happen, i.e. the end of the world.

Accepting that difficulties arise but that they are bearable as long as you are alive.

Accepting that you are fallible and at times you may not get what you want but you remain a worthwhile human being regardless.

Healthy belief = What you want + Keeping it real

In Chapter 2 you learned the reasons why unhealthy beliefs are unhealthy and the difference between healthy and unhealthy beliefs:

- An unhealthy rigid demand or a healthy preference.
- The unhealthy catastrophizing concept and the healthy concept of bad but not the end of the world.
- The unhealthy concept of low frustration tolerance and the healthy high frustration tolerance.
- Unhealthy total self-damning and healthy self-acceptance.

The next thing to do is to modify your unhealthy beliefs to include concepts of external reality and truth in them.

Example: Jane's healthy versions of her unhealthy beliefs

Jane identified the following three unhealthy beliefs:

- I MUST find the diploma easy and not hard. If I find it hard then I won't cope and it will prove I'm stupid.

- I MUST know how I will feel if I need to take time away from my family when I'm doing the diploma. It's awful that

> I don't know and I cannot stand not knowing how I will feel.
>
> - I MUST not take time away from my family during the week to work on my diploma. Doing that would be awful and would prove that I'm a bad mother and wife.

1. Jane's first unhealthy belief

I MUST find the diploma easy. If I find it hard then I won't cope and it will prove that I'm stupid.

This is rigid, inconsistent with reality, illogical and unhelpful. There is no law of the universe that states Jane MUST find the diploma course easy. To demand this would not eradicate the chance that she may find it hard. Just because she would like it to be easy doesn't mean that it HAS to be easy. Her internal insistence that it MUST not be hard causes her to feel anxious.

It is rigid to hold the attitude that she won't cope if she finds the course hard. She is not allowing for any other possibility. Telling herself that she won't cope is not consistent with reality because she won't fall apart if she finds the course hard. It doesn't make sense for Jane to tell herself that she won't cope just because it may be hard and it certainly will not help her to have constructive and healthy thoughts and emotions.

It is rigid to conclude that she is stupid if she finds the course hard. There is no doubt that Jane would be able to prove her intelligence in many different areas and subjects. It doesn't make sense for her to leap to the conclusion that she is a stupid person if she finds the course hard. It just means that she is human and fallible. Being fallible and imperfect is not an indication of her value.

Jane rewrites her first belief by taking each element of the belief and balancing them out.

She keeps the desire but accepts the external reality that there is a chance she may not get it. Instead of I MUST find the diploma easy and not hard, she writes:

I WANT to find the diploma course easy and not hard BUT I accept there is a chance that I might find it hard.

Another version of this might be:

I hope that I find the diploma course easy and not hard BUT that does not mean I MUST find it easy.

She then moves on to the part of low frustration tolerance and balances it out. Instead of telling herself that she will not cope if she finds the course hard, she acknowledges that she may find it hard but that it would not mean that she will not be able to cope. She writes:

If I find the diploma course hard then that would be difficult but it does not mean that I won't cope.

Another version might be:

If I find the diploma course hard then I might be challenged but I will learn to bear it and cope with it.

Jane finally moves on to the part of her belief where she puts herself down by believing that she would be stupid if she finds the course hard. She balances this part by accepting that she is fallible but worthy regardless. She writes:

If I find the course hard it doesn't mean that I am stupid. It just means I am human like everyone else. I remain worthwhile regardless of whether I find the course hard or easy.

Putting all three elements together the healthy belief would be:

I want to find the diploma course easy and not hard BUT I accept there is a chance that I might find it hard. If I find the diploma course hard then that would be difficult but it does not mean that I won't cope. If I find the course hard it doesn't mean that I am stupid. It just means I am human like everyone else. I remain worthwhile regardless of whether I find the course hard or easy.

When she internalizes this new belief she will experience healthy nervousness or concern when she thinks the course may be difficult at times but her healthy belief will keep her focused and confident about her abilities.

2. Jane's second unhealthy belief
I MUST know how I will feel if I need to take time away from my family when I am doing the diploma. It's awful that I don't know and I cannot stand not knowing how I will feel.

Jane's second belief is unhealthy because it is rigid to demand that she MUST know how she will feel. There is no law of the universe that states that she MUST know. It does not allow for the possibility that she may not know how she will feel. At the moment she does not know how she will feel so that is the reality. Telling herself she MUST know does not alter this reality. Jane would dearly love to know how she might feel but this does not mean that she therefore absolutely MUST know. Her demand will not help her. In fact it is causing her more anxiety.

Jane's thinking that it would be awful if she doesn't know is rigid. There are worse things that can happen. It is also not true that it is awful. The world would not end if she did not know. Catastrophizing not knowing doesn't make sense either. It is clear that for Jane, not knowing how she feels would be a bad thing but it doesn't make sense to conclude that it would be awful. Exaggerating the badness of not knowing only makes her feel anxious and so it does not help her.

Jane's belief that she can't cope with not knowing how she feels is rigid and untrue because she is still thinking and writing about it. She is still functioning despite the fact she currently can't imagine how she will feel. It is true that she is feeling stressed and finding not knowing hard but it doesn't make sense to conclude that she is therefore unable to cope. This irrational thinking is not helping her. It is causing her anxiety.

Modifying her belief by balancing it out with reality, Jane now writes the following:

I would like to know how I'd feel if I need to take time away from my family BUT I accept that at the moment I don't.

Another version might be:

I wish I knew how I'd feel if I took time away from my family but that doesn't mean that I absolutely must know.

Jane then modifies the catastrophizing belief by being honest in saying she finds not knowing bad but without exaggerating this badness. Her healthy version now reads:

The fact that I don't know how I will feel if I take time away from my family is bad for me but it is not a catastrophe. The world has not ended.

Jane also modifies her low frustration tolerance belief to its high frustration tolerance version. She understands that 'not knowing how she would feel' is something she finds difficult, however it is something that she can bear. Not knowing will not kill her. The healthy version now reads:

The fact that I don't know how I will feel is difficult but not unbearable. I can tolerate it. I can stand it.

The full healthy belief is:

I wish I knew how I'd feel if I took time away from my family but that doesn't mean that I absolutely must know. The fact that I don't know how I will feel if I take time away from my family is bad for me but it is not a catastrophe. The world has not ended. The fact that I don't know how I will feel is difficult but not unbearable. I can tolerate it. I can stand it.

When Jane internalizes this belief she will feel healthy concern about not knowing in advance how she would feel, but would be able to reason well and calm down. Her healthy belief would stop her feeling anxious.

3. Jane's third unhealthy belief

I MUST not take time away from my family during the week to work on my diploma. Doing that would be awful and it would prove that I'm a bad mother and wife.

It is easy to understand that this belief is rigid and inflexible. Jane's thinking does not allow for any other possibilities that clearly exist in reality. It's not consistent with reality. No law of the universe states that Jane MUST not take time away from her family during the week to work on her diploma because clearly she can. She may not want to do that but that is her choice. There is no sense in concluding that she MUST not take time away from her family just because she would PREFER not to. Her demand would cause guilt and unhappiness, particularly if she ends up taking time away from her family while saying that she MUST not. Her feelings of guilt may even stop her from thinking and making a reasoned decision that, for example, studying may provide her with opportunities that may benefit her family and make for a happier Jane.

Catastrophizing the notion of taking time away from her family is rigid and inflexible. It does not allow for other possibilities to exist. It is neither true nor consistent with reality that taking time away from her family is the worst possible thing, at the moment, when she is imagining herself doing that and feeling the emotion of guilt. When she allows herself to reason properly she can see that worse things can happen, so taking time away from her family is not the worst thing even though she considers it to be bad. Jane considers taking this additional time away to be a bad thing but it does not make sense to conclude that it is awful. This will only cause greater feelings of guilt and unhappiness.

Finally, Jane's conclusion that she would be a bad mother and wife if she took time away from her family is rigid and inflexible. It offers no other possibilities for her. It offers no hope of ever being anything else, like 'not such a bad mother', or even a 'good mother'. It is not true that she would become a bad mother and wife as a direct result of her actions. If this were true then she would be a bad mother and wife in everything else that she does as a mother and a wife.

To conclude that her action of taking time away from her family implies she is a bad mother and wife does not make sense. Her total self-damning will cause feelings of guilt and negative thoughts. She will be feeling wretched every time she sits down to study – hardly a formula for success if she decides to apply for the diploma. All it proves is that she is human and fallible, like everyone else.

Once again, Jane understands the destructive nature of the unhealthy belief as well as understanding that it is not true.

She balances it out with reality by making it flexible so that she allows herself to express her preference without being rigid about it. Her preference is:

It would be wonderful if I didn't have to take time away from my family during the week to study, but I accept that I might have to. It doesn't mean that I absolutely MUST not do it.

She acknowledges that because it is something that she thinks would be a bad thing for her, she would need to express it. However, she realizes that she does not need to exaggerate how bad it would be. She then writes:

I won't like it when I take time away because I think it will be bad but not awful.

Finally, she tackles the self-damning belief. She acknowledges that her actions are not an indication of her value as a mother and wife. There are so many other opportunities for quality time. She writes:

It would not make me a bad mother and wife if I took time away to study, because I'm human and I am a worthwhile and valuable mother, even if I'm not totally perfect. No one is. I accept myself.

Putting all these elements together Jane's healthy belief would be:

It would be wonderful if I didn't have to take time away from my family during the week to study but I accept that I might have to and it doesn't mean that I absolutely MUST not do it. I won't like it when I take time away because I think it will be bad but not awful. It would not make me a bad mother and wife if I took time away to study, because I'm human and I am a worthwhile and valuable mother, even if I'm not totally perfect. No one is. I accept myself.

When Jane internalizes this belief she will feel healthy remorse when she takes time away to study. However, she will still be able to study because she will have thoughts that remind her that it is her choice. She will be able to think of positive things to do to make up for the time she spends away. She will eventually be able to think of the long-term and short-term benefits.

Exercise

Write down your unhealthy beliefs.

Take each belief and each element of it and think about why it is unhealthy.

Tip: Why is the 'MUST' unhealthy? Why is catastrophizing badness unhealthy? Why is low frustration tolerance unhealthy? Why is self-, other- or world-damning unhealthy?

Write the healthy version for each of your beliefs. Think about what healthy negative emotions you would feel and what the belief would cause once you have internalized it.

Tip: Healthy negative emotions are, for example, concern instead of anxiety, remorse instead of guilt, annoyance instead of anger.

Personally persuasive reasons – what's in it for me?

So far you have learned how to set goals that are significant to you and reflect on the emotions that have blocked you from taking action. You then explored and identified the unhealthy and irrational beliefs that were causing each of the different unhealthy emotions. You reflected on why your unhealthy beliefs were unhealthy and then wrote their healthy versions. All of this has helped you to use reasoned thinking.

Reasoned thinking enables you to see that there is a better and healthier way to use your mind. This frees you to make choices rather than having a sense that your hands are tied and that this is how you are and how life is. Healthy beliefs give you back your accountability. When you are accountable for your life you are free because you are making choices based on healthy thinking rather than irrational and unrealistic thinking that makes you miserable, scared and avoidant. Effectively your choices will emerge out of good quality truth and emotions rather than self-deprecation and feelings of anxiety and depression. You can clarify your emotions, make your decision and see whether you really want to go for your goals or not.

This section continues the process of reflection but this time you will learn to think of personal reasons *in favour of your healthy beliefs* and personal reasons *against your unhealthy beliefs*. This will expand on the theory of the last section. You are now getting into more detail and injecting some energy and passion into your goal. You will be asking yourself:

- What's in it for me?
- What's in it for me in committing to and strengthening my healthy beliefs?
- What's in it for me in keeping my unhealthy beliefs?

This will help strengthen your healthy beliefs and weaken your unhealthy ones. When you can see how you will benefit you are more likely to commit yourself, otherwise you would be unlikely to convince yourself to do it or to focus on it. Your 'what's in it for me' reasons will begin to motivate you towards your goal. It makes sense in so many different areas of life. Think of something that you look forward to, like going on a holiday. If you didn't see any benefits to you personally in going on holiday, the chances of your going become remote.

So what's in it for you in believing that you are a worthwhile but fallible human being? What images does this statement generate in your mind? What feelings does it cause you to have? How does it affect the way that you hold yourself? How would you talk to yourself? What would other people see if you believed it?

You can see how your mind begins to work as you allow yourself to reflect on these questions. You can definitely see there is something in it for you: happiness, confidence and an increased likelihood of success and achievement. That's what is in it for you ultimately.

Your 'what's in it for me' lists will be used in the process of your goal achievement to help you to stay focused on what you want. The negative list belonging to 'what's in it for me' in keeping the unhealthy beliefs will be used when you are putting in effort, or when you feel like giving up.

Exercise

Start this exercise by writing down your healthy beliefs, one at a time. Think of all the positive personal benefits that would accrue if you truly believed your healthy statement. What would be in it for you in believing your healthy belief in the short and in the long term?

Write down the unhealthy beliefs, one at a time, and think about what benefits you get from keeping the unhealthy beliefs. Hopefully, you will see that you derive very few, and definitely none that help you achieve your important goals. This will show all the negative consequences to you personally in keeping these limiting beliefs.

Example

Assume that a man has identified the following unhealthy and healthy belief.

Unhealthy belief

People must not judge me negatively when they meet me. If they do, it's awful, unbearable and proves I'm unworthy.

Healthy belief

I'd really like it if people did not judge me negatively when they meet me but that does not mean they *must* not judge me negatively either. If they do, it would be bad but not the end of the world. It would be tough but not unbearable. It would not mean I'm unworthy. I'm fallible, some people will like me and some might not. I remain worthwhile regardless because my worth does not depend on people's negative or positive judgement.

What's in it for me in keeping my unhealthy belief?

- It makes me feel anxious.
- I'm not myself in the company of other people.
- I worry about what to say.
- I worry about how I'm saying things.
- It stops me from engaging.
- I'm focused on my feelings and not on the conversation.
- It makes my hands shake.
- It makes me sweat and go red.
- It makes me feel clumsy.
- I run out of things to say.

- I end up agreeing with everything people say even if I disagree in my head.
- It makes me end up talking to people I don't want to talk to.
- I end up declining invitations.
- It affects my social life badly.
- It makes me unhappy.
- It makes me withdraw from conversations because I'm thinking about whether they like me or not.
- I say things like 'oh, I see', and 'really, that's so funny' even when it isn't.
- It makes me feel that I'm bad and not normal.

What's in it for me in strengthening my healthy belief?

- I would feel more relaxed and not anxious.
- I would be me.
- I would enjoy myself more.
- I would allow people to know me.
- People will probably like me because I'm being me.
- I will feel strong and cope if someone does not like me. That's life.
- I will express what I think and feel better.
- I will agree when I agree with someone.
- I will disagree when I disagree with someone.
- I will be focused on the conversation and on the people I'm talking to.
- I will get a better sense about other people because I won't be in my head all the time.
- My hands won't shake.
- I will be cool and comfortable.
- I will feel that I have a right just like everyone else.

- I will like myself.
- I will be open and happy.
- I will feel more confident in my self.
- I will have good conversations and be able to chat up someone I fancy.
- I will be relaxed and laugh and joke freely.
- I will be great. ☺

Exercise

Write down your first unhealthy belief and come up with 10 to 20 reasons why it's no good for you personally.

Write down your first healthy belief and come up with at least 10 to 20 'what's in it for me' reasons why your healthy belief would be good for you personally.

Repeat the above for each of your other unhealthy and healthy beliefs.

CHAPTER 4

Obstacles to goal achievement

This chapter explains what we experience when setting goals. All our old habits and attitudes resurface from our subconscious mind, sometimes in reaction to other people's attitudes and assumptions. The following topics will help you overcome obstacles and remain focused on your goal.

- Emotional obstacles
- Habitual or behavioural obstacles
- Environmental obstacles
- Cognitive (thinking) obstacles

Tolerating tension and discomfort

Tension and discomfort are natural and even necessary as we set goals and then strive to achieve them. At this stage many people give up because they focus on the tension instead of the end result.

Why do we feel tension and discomfort when we want to change?

Tension and discomfort are necessary feelings in the process of achieving your goal. In fact, if you do not experience them then the goal is either not important or not what you really want.

Focusing on the goal

This is about making the goal the focus of your thoughts on a daily and regular basis.

How to tolerate the natural discomfort

The persuasive reasons you listed earlier come into their own now. This topic is about using the ammunition of 'what's in it for me' and other techniques to tolerate the natural tension. At this stage the tension can be reframed and called 'natural excitement'.

Obstacles to goal achievement

In this chapter you will learn what happens when you set significant goals and commit to them. You are goal-striving by nature, so setting goals and wanting what is important to you is natural. You also know that most of the time you act in accordance with your beliefs, which cause your emotions, behaviours and thoughts. If your belief is un- healthy, your emotions, thoughts and behaviours, your performance and therefore goal achievement will match. Besides the immediate emotional obstacles that you identified in Chapter 3, other emotional, cognitive, habitual and environmental issues become evident.

Think about what happens when you set a significant goal, for example, going on holiday, buying a car, renting or buying property or simply thinking about buying a vacuum cleaner.

The day before you decide that you want to buy something important, the thought of the item will not have been in your conscious mind. However, as soon as you say to yourself, 'I want to buy X', immediately you become like a detective. Suddenly your antennae is switched on. You start to become aware of words, pictures, ideas, sounds and emotions related to what you want to buy.

For example, if you decide to rent or buy property, you see 'For Sale' signs everywhere you go. If you think of going on holiday, you take notice of TV adverts for exotic destinations; you become aware of travel agents on your way to work. If you want to buy a vacuum cleaner, you notice them in department stores and shops. If you are thinking about having children, you begin to see pregnant women and children everywhere.

All these things that you become conscious of were there anyway, but as soon as you say 'I want to ...' your mind makes you conscious of those things that are related to your goal. Your mind is programmed to strive towards what you want and the things that are important to you so you can attain them and feel happier than you did before. You could say that your mind is your friend, looking after you and helping you towards your goal as long as you are striving towards your desires, as long as you are making choices based on what you want.

However, as soon as any negative, unhealthy 'have to' demands appear, or as soon as any 'end of the world', awful, terrible, catastrophizing, or 'I can't cope', low frustration tolerance beliefs are triggered, it's another story.

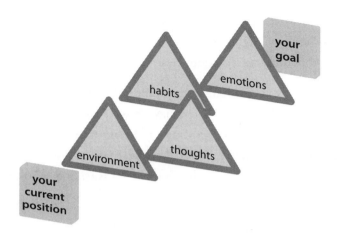

This happens because catastrophizing beliefs and low frustration tolerance beliefs tell your mind that you will, essentially, perish. They cause unhealthy negative emotions that say 'run and save your bacon'. So when you set and commit yourself to a significant healthy **SMART** goal, emotional, habitual, cognitive and environmental obstacles are triggered like hurdles in a 100-metre race. You now have a choice of getting over the hurdles and running towards the finishing line or staying behind the hurdles and looking at the finishing line from your current position.

Emotional obstacles

You have already identified unhealthy negative emotions, such as anxiety or guilt, that you became aware of as soon as you set your goal and declared it important.

Unless you change these emotions then you will find it difficult to focus on your goal in a positive way. It will feel like someone is holding onto you as you are trying to walk.

You may have an emotion about an emotion or a problem about a problem. You may, for example, have an anxiety about your anxiety. This is more commonly known as fear of fear. You may also have depression about your anxiety, or anger about your anxiety. So you see, people can disturb themselves about anything.

You will recall that healthy beliefs cause healthy negative emotions like concern or annoyance as opposed to unhealthy emotions such as anxiety and anger. However, it is also possible that you can create a problem about a healthy negative emotion.

Because healthy negative emotions can feel uncomfortable, you may think it is wrong to feel them or assume that it's an indication that you are not strong enough. However, when you feel healthy nervousness it is absolutely appropriate. When you commit yourself to a goal that you care about you may feel a healthy negative emotion that will be mixed with a sense of excitement. This healthy but negative emotion is natural. Do not assume that there is something wrong and start worrying about it. If that happens then you may create an unhealthy negative state in response to what was a healthy negative state to begin with.

This could happen at the beginning of goal setting, when you commit to your goal or when you start taking action to achieve your goal. Therefore, you need to watch that you do not create an emotional problem about feeling healthy tension and nervousness.

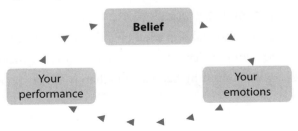

Once you start moving towards your goal, you will open yourself up to what can happen in life. You may be dealing with people, deadlines, making decisions, or considering a number of options. You will open yourself up to things that both are within and outside your control.

Your emotional response will influence your performance and success. And what do you think will be causing your emotional state? It will of course be your beliefs, whether healthy or unhealthy.

Example

Jonathan is a 45-year-old man who, after much thought, started an IT business with two partners. He worked through his initial anxiety about whether he could do it by identifying and accepting that he was anxious. He replaced his unhealthy belief by its healthy version and strengthened it through cognitive and behavioural techniques. He has now been self-employed for a year and is focused on and committed to his goal. One of the emotions that Jonathan experiences is anger towards one of his business partners, which started soon after they began working together. Jonathan has found this surprising because in his previous jobs he was much more tolerant with work colleagues. He hides it well but seethes deep down and is usually less engaging with this particular partner. His anger is beginning to trouble him and he is now becoming worried that it could jeopardize their business relationship.

Jonathan's emotional obstacles

Jonathan has two emotional obstacles. He feels anger towards one of his business partners and anxiety about the potential consequences of his anger. The anger is unhealthy because Jonathan is not acting assertively and expressing how he is feeling about whatever his business partner is or is not doing. Instead he is demonstrating his anger in a passive but aggressive way by not engaging as much with his business partner. The reason he is not being honest about his emotion is because he is worried that he would say things in an inappropriate way which in turn may affect the business relationship.

Jonathan's emotional obstacles have arisen because he is committed to his goal of starting (and then running) a new business. This important goal has triggered emotions which he did not experience in his previous jobs. His new business is more important to him.

Unless Jonathan resolves these emotional obstacles, he will end up increasing the chances of inappropriate and destructive outbursts.

Jonathan's solution

Jonathan decides to identify the unhealthy belief causing his unhealthy anger by applying the ABC model. The 'A' is the trigger, so he recalls the most significant incident when he felt angry with his business partner and then asks himself the following:

What do my feelings of anger tell me about what I am demanding from my business partner?

He concludes that he is demanding that his business partner be as organized as he is.

Jonathan also identifies that he has been labelling his business partner as 'inefficient' because he is not as organized.

He then rewrites this unhealthy belief as follows:

I would really like it if my business partner were as organized as me, but he does not HAVE to be. The fact that he is not does not mean he is an inefficient person. He's not perfect but neither am I. He is a worthwhile person regardless of the fact that he is less organized. He definitely has other strengths too.

Jonathan then considers what's in it for him in strengthening his healthy belief or in keeping his unhealthy belief about his business partner.

This process helps Jonathan to gain insight about why he was feeling so angry and now realizes how to correct what he believed about his partner.

Gossiping, bitching and communication problems

When you begin to experience unhealthy negative emotional obstacles following your commitment to your positive goal, it is important that you begin to find an appropriate and healthy way of dealing with them. Unresolved emotional obstacles will lead you to avoid communicating your feelings effectively. They may cause you to withhold information from others. You may start to relate to others in unhealthy ways, for example you may begin to put them down, gossip behind their backs and generally defocus from solving the problem you are experiencing.

For example, Jonathan recognizes that his feelings of anxiety about potential conflict, if he expresses anger or disagreement, are preventing him from talking to his business partner about being more organized. He realizes that unless he learns to change his feelings of anxiety he will remain unassertive in his new business. Clearly if Jonathan remains anxious about displaying any annoyance he will be unable to express his opinions about events at work. This in turn may cause him unhappiness and he might even start withholding information or putting his business partner down in front of other people. The long-term effect of such an emotional position results in more negative outcomes and communication problems.

Jonathan recognizes his demand that the business must not be affected detrimentally if he talks to his partner about being more organized because that would be awful and he would not be able to cope with it.

Jonathan writes his healthy belief as follows:

I'd really like not to end up with detrimental business problems when I talk to my partner about being more organized, but I accept that such a possibility exists. If it happens, it would be really bad but it won't be a world disaster; it would be very unfortunate and difficult but I would be able to cope and deal with it somehow.

Jonathan then makes a list of 'what's in it for me' in believing the above instead of the previously demanding version.

As you can see, the first thing is that this belief frees Jonathan to talk to his business partner. He is no longer in that state of anxiety which causes avoidance and communication problems. Working on his first belief that caused anger will mean that Jonathan will be able to express his feelings and thoughts in an appropriate way. His first healthy belief will cause him to be as appropriate as he can be. His second healthy belief will allow him to do it.

Exercise

Reflect on the emotional obstacles you became aware of when you committed yourself to your significant goal, for example, anxiety, anger, guilt, envy.

Identify the unhealthy belief for each emotional obstacle by asking yourself what your feelings were telling you about your demands. Ask yourself about the consequences if your demand is not met. Do your feelings tell you it would be awful, unbearable or that you are unworthy?

Write down the healthy versions of your unhealthy emotional obstacles.

Example: I want to xyz but I don't have to xyz. If I don't it would be bad but not terrible, difficult or unbearable; I'm not unworthy. I'm fallible and my worth does not depend on anything. It's inside me.

Write the 'what's in it for me' reasons for focusing on the healthy belief and the 'what's in it for me' reasons for focusing your energy on the unhealthy beliefs that are causing your emotional obstacles.

Habitual and behavioural obstacles

Habitual and behavioural obstacles are hurdles that you can become aware of when you set and commit yourself to a significant goal.

Commitment to achieving a goal requires you to be motivated, positive, forward-looking, resilient and focused. This means that your goal takes priority over many of your habits and certain comforts. Your goal needs to be not just important, but more important than other things in your life.

Habits are learned behaviours and actions that have been repeated and rehearsed so many times that they become automatic and feel effortless. They are stored in the subconscious part of the mind, so you don't consciously think about them, you just do them because you are so used to them.

Habits can be good, bad or neutral

Good habits include knowing what your name is or the names of your friends and colleagues, driving your car well or cycling. If your brain did not have this ability to learn and store what you have learned, you would always be having to think about how to do things. When you first start taking driving lessons, for example, you are conscious of how bad you are at driving and everything feels like an effort. You concentrate hard and try to remember what your driving instructor is telling you: mirror, check, signal, check, manoeuvre, check. You are very conscious of everything you are doing. In other words, you are consciously incompetent.

As you keep practising and showing up for your driving lessons you begin to feel more capable. You are still consciously learning and extremely aware of your surroundings and other cars on the road. You are consciously putting into practice what you are learning, but it still does not feel effortless. You are now consciously competent.

Then you pass your driving test and are driving on your own to work and to the supermarket. One day you realize that you have not consciously thought: mirror, signal, manoeuvre. In fact you have been listening to the radio and smiling or singing to yourself. Now, you are unconsciously competent. Driving has now become a habit.

You may also unconsciously begin to believe that you are the best driver ever and start racing others on the road. You are now speedily moving into becoming unconsciously incompetent as a driver. If something unfortunate happens, you start the whole process of re-evaluating your skills and reflecting on what you have learned over again.

It is easy to see how habits can develop. The same process can happen with something negative, like being late for appointments, eating everything on your plate even when you are full, or driving everywhere, even to the corner shop. When you commit yourself to a significant goal, you may become aware of habits that stand between you and your goal. Will you keep the habit or the goal? If your goal is important then you keep the goal and learn a new habit by stopping the one that is causing the obstacle.

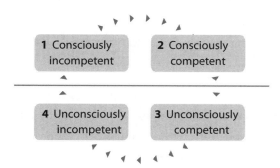

Example

Maggie is a 29-year-old woman who works in a bank and enjoys socializing several times a week with her friends. Usually they go to a bar or a club, drink a lot of alcohol and have a good time. She recently started to exercise and watch her diet. She decided to lose 10 pounds in weight. She is doing well with both her food intake and the exercising, but the weight is not coming off as quickly as she had planned. She realizes that her social drinking is an obstacle; as soon as she is with friends she automatically says yes to offers of drinks and partying. She feels as though she is on auto-pilot. The next day she remembers that she really needs to take more control and stick to her goal. It is only then that she becomes aware of letting go of her goal. She could of course compensate by exercising more and eating less but she recognizes that would not be a healthy path to take.

Maggie's habitual obstacle

Maggie's habit of social drinking a few times a week is working against her goal of weight loss. This is a habit because she automatically and unconsciously falls into the same behaviour of accepting drinks without consciously thinking about what she is doing or keeping her goal in mind. This in turn maintains the habit and she loses sight of her goal. She will find it difficult to lose the extra 10 pounds without changing or modifying her social drinking habit.

Maggie became aware of her habitual social drinking once she declared her weight loss goal as significant and started to implement her plan. Up to that point social drinking was not an issue for her.

Maggie's solution

Maggie decides to keep her goal in mind and have only a couple of drinks when she goes out.

She notices that she begins to feel tension in her body when she starts to say 'no' and usually ends up having more drinks.

She reflects on what she feels in her body when she refuses a drink. She becomes aware that the tension is actually similar to a feeling of anxiety.

She asks herself what her feelings are telling her about her demands when she is saying no to alcohol. She understands that she is demanding that she MUST have the drink right now and that she can't stand not having one like everyone else. In that moment she is also letting go of her significant goal of losing weight.

She considers this unhealthy belief that is causing her problems with changing her habit and she rewrites it as follows:

I would like to have a drink right now but I don't have to. The fact that I'm choosing not to have one is uncomfortable but I can stand not having a drink. I want to lose the 10 pounds.

This new belief is helpful and constructive. It reminds Maggie that it is her choice to reduce her drinking and that she is doing it because she wants to achieve her desired goal. She realizes that she can continue to drink but she would then modify or give up on her goal. She is aware that no one is holding a gun to her head to force her to drink. She does not have to drink just because everyone else is drinking. It is her choice to do what she wants. She wants to lose weight so she chooses to reduce her drinking despite the discomfort of seeing everyone else drinking.

She helps herself to feel more motivated about her choice by writing down a list of 'what's in it for me' in adopting the healthy belief as opposed to the unhealthy demand.

The example illustrates that when you start changing a habit you will feel tension in your body because you are giving up one thing that feels 'natural' and automatic, in favour of something new that you are not used to. Unless you then work on the belief that is causing the tension and write its healthy version, the chances of giving in to the habitual obstacle increase.

Exercise

Reflect on the habits that you feel will or have become an obstacle to your goal achievement, for example lying down in front of the TV instead of writing letters to potential customers.

Start by changing the habits and notice what you feel in your body. If you find that you have been giving in to your old habits, identify the emotion and tension you felt when you tried to change the habit.

Identify what your emotions were telling you about what you were demanding when you started to change the habit, for example: 'I must watch TV and feel comfortable'.

Become aware of what your feelings were telling you when you stopped the habit. Did they tell you it's terrible or that you can't stand not doing the habitual thing?

Write the healthy version of the unhealthy habitual belief.

Write a list of 'what's in it for me' in focusing on the healthy belief, and 'what's in it for me' in keeping the unhealthy habitual belief in terms of your goal achievement.

Cognitive obstacles

Cognitive obstacles are particularly unhelpful attitudes and thoughts that you become aware of when you commit yourself to your goal, or when you are taking action and moving towards your goal. They are hurdles that appear once you have focused on your goal.

They get triggered because plans involving your goal may, for example, require you to talk to certain people, put yourself forward for events or make telephone calls.

The attitude you take can either help or hinder you when you have a goal in mind. Clearly, a negative, judgemental or prejudiced attitude will not set you up for success and may stop you in your pursuit of your goal.

An appropriate attitude is one of the key ingredients in goal achievement. Your attitude towards something or someone can be a function of how you feel about yourself, about other people or about the world. It is related to how you think things should or should not be.

A healthy, optimistic and encouraging attitude comes from a position of strength and acceptance of people and their differences. It comes from being flexible and seeing that other ways and alternative solutions are possible.

When it comes to your goals it is important that you have a strong focus and a flexible, helpful and positive attitude. If you find that you don't then you can always change your attitude and keep your goal.

Example

Stuart works in sales and is ambitious. He usually manages to do well and, together with his colleagues, reports to the sales manager every Monday morning. The sales manager reviews the overall team objectives and agrees individual and team targets. As part of the team objectives, he asks everyone to work together to come up with some creative and 'outside the box' solutions to increasing sales.

During the brainstorming session, Stuart is criticized for having a glib attitude. He is told that he behaves in a dismissive way towards certain colleagues and ideas. He is asked to come to the next meeting with a different attitude.

After some initial discomfort Stuart begins to reflect on this.

Stuart's cognitive obstacle

If you work in a team you can have a positive, open and encouraging attitude towards certain ideas and solutions, or you can be dismissive, sarcastic or belittling. The first attitude will encourage a sense of relaxation and fun during the exercise but the latter will trigger resentment, self-consciousness and reserve.

Stuart's glib attitude was criticized because it was not helpful in meeting the objectives, i.e. coming up with creative solutions. It was hindering the process. He was not aware of his attitude until it was pointed out to him.

A sarcastic or belittling attitude is a smokescreen for low self-esteem. In Stuart's example, his attitude demonstrated his own low self-esteem. In attempting to belittle or dismiss others, he was trying to elevate himself above them, but in a dysfunctional way. His colleagues and his boss noticed this and his attitude did not work in his favour.

Stuart's solution

When Stuart reflected on his attitude, recalled his response to his colleagues and asked himself why he had responded in that way, he became aware that he wanted to be seen as the brightest and most creative member of the team. He recalled that he felt tense in the moments when he didn't have a new idea and revelled in his positive feelings when he did. He recalled that his attitude was dismissive when he experienced both the positive feelings and the negative tension.

He realized that he felt pangs of anxiety when he did not have creative ideas while others did. He asked himself what his feelings told him about what he was demanding when he did not have creative ideas. He identified a demand that he absolutely MUST be acknowledged as having the most creative ideas among his colleagues; otherwise, it would mean he was a failure.

Stuart realized that he was dismissing himself if others did not view him as the most creative during the meeting. His own self dismissal was causing him to have a dismissive attitude towards his colleagues.

He reconstructed his belief to its healthy version:

I'd prefer to have my colleagues acknowledge me as the most creative one, but they absolutely do not have to. If they don't it doesn't mean I'm a failure. I am worthy but fallible, like everyone.

Stuart began to write his 'what's in it for me' reasons for adopting the healthy belief as opposed to his current unhealthy belief. He began to see that his healthy belief would cause a change in his attitude when he was with his colleagues. His healthy belief would stop his dismissive attitude because he would begin to value rather than dismiss himself.

Exercise

Think about your goal and reflect on your attitude. Write down any negative or ambivalent attitudes you have become aware of.

Identify your unhealthy belief that is supporting your negative attitude. (Work out your demands and any awfulizing, low frustration tolerance and self/other/world-damning beliefs.)

Write the healthy version of your unhealthy beliefs.

Write the 'what's in it for me' reasons to keep the healthy belief and 'what's in it for me' in keeping the unhealthy belief.

How would your healthy belief change your attitude?

Implement the change in attitude!

Environmental obstacles

Environmental obstacles are associated with your surroundings. They are all the unhelpful factors or hurdles at home or in the office.

How conducive is your environment to achieving your goal? While any long lasting change comes from a change in your beliefs, it is smart to reflect on how you can make your environment work for you instead of against you when it comes to your goal.

For example, if your goal is weight loss, having a cupboard full of biscuits adds an unnecessary obstacle that increases your chances of giving in to temptation. You need to make your home work with you.

If you live with your partner or family, then their support would be helpful. It is not essential but having the right type of support makes for an easier life. It may be useful to ask for support from your family, but remember it is about asking, not demanding or needing the support.

If you can influence your environment to work for you in terms of your goal, it would make sense to do so. If environmental changes are outside your control you will need to strengthen your tolerance and keep focused on your goal.

Exercise

List the environmental obstacles that are in your control. Begin to change them to work with your goal.

List environmental factors outside your control. Identify the healthy attitudes and beliefs that would enable you to remain focused on your goal despite the environmental obstacles.

Tolerating tension and discomfort

Why do we feel tension and discomfort when we want to change?

You know when you are outside your comfort zone because your body naturally gives out signals that you are tense and uncomfortable. The degree of discomfort you feel is caused by your beliefs and attitude about difficulty. Typically these are low frustration beliefs, thoughts and speech such as 'I can't cope', 'this is intolerable' and 'I can't stand this'. You can become tense about feeling tension. You may say 'I can't stand stress' or 'I need to be comfortable'. Have you noticed that these demands may cause you to become more tense and anxious?

As you know, your beliefs represent what you think of yourself and of your abilities. They function like an automatic pilot. Setting a goal means you want to move from one position to a more satisfactory one. If you wish to lose weight or become confident at giving presentations, your current beliefs may cause you to feel anxiety, tension and have thoughts like, 'I'm not good enough' or, 'I can't do it'. They will also cause you to act in accordance with what you believe and think. You now understand that none of these thoughts are true, but your automatic pilot has been set to cause them anyway and as soon as you attempt to change, the automatic pilot switches on, causing your negative thoughts and emotions.

This is not your fault and doesn't mean that you are weak or doing something wrong. It's part of the natural process of change. Your current unhealthy belief is trying to maintain its position because it is strong. If you think and act in accordance with what the belief is telling you, you will continue to strengthen its position even though it is not based on any truth, common sense or benefit.

It is easy to understand emotional and physical tension if you think about your currently held unhealthy belief as an energy box that is radiating emotions, negative or limiting thoughts, and causing unhelpful behavioural tendencies and behaviours as well as physical symptoms.

An unhealthy belief causes feelings like worry or anxiety, behaviours like avoidance or passivity, and negative thoughts like 'I can't do it', 'I've always failed', 'I won't be able to manage it' or 'it's impossible for me make it work and change'. You may experience physical symptoms like sweating, headaches or blushing. It has been reinforced through years of conditioning and repetition, causing you to believe that there is something weak or flawed about you. You now know that this belief is unhelpful but knowing it does not alter what it makes you feel, do and think. Each time you have these negative thoughts, justify them and act as if they are true, their energy is fed back into the belief, causing the energy box to radiate with even more power.

You can choose to make a change now by understanding the healthy version of your currently held unhealthy belief. The new belief is like a tiny glow that you want to become more powerful than the habitual, strong, unhealthy one. For it to start radiating positive feelings, thoughts and behaviours automatically, you need to energize it with constructive, positive, helpful thoughts and behaviours. Only then will you be in a position to change and radiate feelings of confidence. For the process to work, repetition of your healthy goal is vital.

The following diagram illustrates this process:

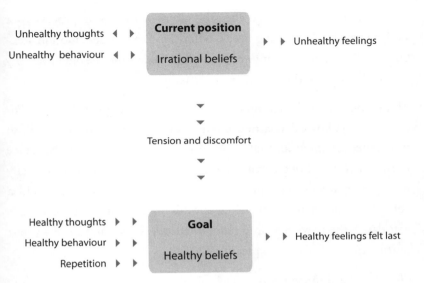

If you attempt to energize the healthy belief with new constructive thoughts and behaviour so that, in time, it radiates healthy feelings, but at the same time continue to entertain unhealthy thoughts and behaviours because you are feeling the negative emotions that radiate from them, it's like giving yourself something good with one hand and then throwing it away with the other. This means healthy emotional change is unlikely to happen.

So how do you make this change?

- *You start thinking in a constructive way and challenge the unhealthy negative thoughts.*
- *You start behaving in a constructive way and stop behaving in an unhealthy way.*
- *You repeat the above over and over again whilst tolerating the unhealthy negative emotions until …*
- *Your feelings change … at last.*

When your feelings change after the effort of the above process your healthy belief will be firing on all cylinders. The healthy emotional energy will be strong and reinforce the healthy belief, and the old unhealthy belief will be starved of its emotional energy.

Think about any change process you have already gone through. For example, you learned a particular dance and have practised it enough so now it feels natural and effortless. You learn that some of the dance movements you thought you were good at were, in reality, technically wrong. You are shown the proper dance steps. You now have a better idea about how you should be dancing, but this does not automatically make you dance the new steps in a natural, effortless way. You need to start putting the new steps into practice.

How do you think you would feel initially? Would you feel completely natural or uncomfortably clumsy? You might feel a natural tendency to revert back to the wrong steps, but if you did that then no change would happen. You would need to keep practising the new steps while tolerating the urge to dance in the old but incorrect way, until the new steps feel natural and automatic.

The same analogy applies if you find out that the way you hold your snooker cue is wrong, or the way you sing or play music is wrong. You go through the same process of relearning the new skill until it feels like a habit.

It's exactly the same with changing beliefs. You are literally changing one habit into another, better habit. So please remember your feelings will change and that this will last – the new belief becomes the new way and the unhealthy belief is the old way and no longer instinctive or automatic.

Focusing on the goal

Your healthy belief is the foundation that supports you in achieving your goal. Your goal is the end result; it's the thing that you want. It's what you want to achieve. So it should be exciting when you imagine yourself with your goal achieved.

If you focus on the discomfort of change instead of your goal, you will take your attention off the end result. Your goal needs to be at the front of your mind, not something you remember every now and then.

Think of a 100 metre hurdle runner with his eye on the finish line as he runs towards it, jumping over the hurdles that are in his way. If he focused on the hurdle instead of the finish line, he would crash straight into it and fail.

It's important that you make your goal the focus of your healthy thoughts on a daily basis. The more often you think of the end result, the more likely you will maintain the momentum to do the necessary work to make it happen. When you take your attention off your goal, you let go of what you want to achieve. Taking time to think of your goal only takes a matter of seconds but it is extremely important.

For example, if your goal is to get your weight down to a particular point, or to slim down to a smaller dress or trouser size, then bringing this image to your mind every day will help. Think of the end result when you wake up, before you have your breakfast, lunch and dinner, and every time you eat something.

You can apply this to any goal. All you need to do is to see the end result daily and as often as you can.

How to tolerate the natural discomfort

So far you've learned that healthy beliefs are the foundation behind goal achievement. You know that the process of change and moving towards your goal feels uncomfortable because you are putting into practice healthy thinking and healthy behaviour, which initially feels unusual or unnatural. You can disempower an unhealthy belief by not giving in to the emotions that it causes you as you put your healthy thinking and behaviour into action.

You have also learned that when you set a goal, other cognitive, habitual, emotional and environmental factors can kick in. So in order to keep moving towards your goal, you can find ways to deal with these obstacles by identifying the unhealthy beliefs that cause them, understanding healthy alternative beliefs and finding ways to overcome the obstacles rather than sabotaging the goal.

You've learned that you need to be thinking and imagining your goal on a daily and regular basis to keep you moving in the right direction.

Is there a way to tolerate the natural discomfort you experience when you stretch your comfort zone and start moving towards your goal?

One of the best ways is to use the ammunition of the 'what's in it for me' reasons. You can go over these each day. Coupled with the daily focus on your goal, these will give you the momentum to move through the discomfort of change in a positive and healthy manner. It's like giving yourself a daily shot of positive excitement before you do the work necessary for your goal.

You can now see that what you would have called discomfort, or being out of your comfort zone, can be viewed as excitement and energy which you need. It's the fuel that propels you into action.

To sum up: focusing on your goal and your healthy belief daily, challenging the unhealthy thoughts, recalling and reciting your 'what's in it for me' reasons, and finally viewing the discomfort of change as natural excitement, you will have the strong mind necessary for your goal achievement. The work and the effort do not feel so daunting now.

Example

Remember the example in Chapter 3 of 'what's in it for me' reasons.

Assume that a man identifies the following unhealthy and healthy belief.

People must not judge me negatively when they meet me. If they do, it's awful, unbearable, and proves I'm unworthy.

He turns this into a healthy belief:

I'd really like it if people did not judge me negatively when they meet me, but that does not mean they MUST not judge me negatively either. If they do, it would be bad but not the end of the world. It would be tough but not unbearable. It would not mean I'm unworthy. I'm fallible; some people will like me and some might not but I remain worthwhile regardless, because my worth does not depend on people's negative or indeed positive judgement.

You can easily understand that the main goal for this man is to be confident and calm when he is in social situation.

What's in it for me in keeping my unhealthy belief?

- It makes me feel anxious.
- I'm not myself in the company of other people.
- I worry about what to say.
- I worry about how I'm saying things.
- It stops me from engaging.
- I'm focused on my feelings and not on the conversation.
- It makes my hands shake.
- It makes me sweat and go red.
- It makes me feel clumsy.
- I run out of things to say.
- I agree with everything people say even if I disagree.
- It makes me talk to people I don't want to talk to.
- I end up declining invitations.
- It affects my social life badly.
- It makes me unhappy.
- It makes me withdraw from conversations because I'm thinking about whether they like me or not.
- I say things like 'oh I see', or 'really, that's so funny' even when it isn't.
- It makes me feel that I'm not normal.

What's in it for me in strengthening my healthy belief?

- I would feel more relaxed and not anxious.
- I would be me.
- I would enjoy myself more.
- I would allow people to know me.

- People would probably like me because I'm being me.
- I will feel strong and cope if someone does not like me. That's life.
- I will express what I think and feel better.
- I will agree when I agree with someone.
- I will disagree when I disagree with someone.
- I will be focused on the conversation and on the people I'm talking to.
- I will get a better sense about other people because I won't be in my head all the time.
- My hands won't shake.
- I will be cool and comfortable.
- I will feel that I have a right just like everyone else.
- I will like myself.
- I will be open and happy.
- I will feel more confident in my self.
- I will have good conversations and be able to chat up someone I fancy.
- I will be relaxed and laugh and joke freely.
- I will be great. ☺

What he will do on a daily basis

Each day, he will recall his goal and imagine himself in accordance with his goal. He will also rehearse his healthy belief. He will go through his 'what's in it for me' reasons to help him remember why he is continuing to stretch his comfort zone by socializing and repeating his healthy belief. He can now rename these feelings of discomfort as natural excitement.

Exercise

Go over what you have done so far and write your overall goal, followed by the unhealthy and healthy beliefs. Make a list of 'what's in it for me' underneath your beliefs.

Every day, read and imagine that your goal is achieved.

Rehearse your healthy goal and go over your 'what's in it for me' reasons.

Rename any feelings of discomfort you experience as 'natural excitement'.

CHAPTER 5

Developing cognitive skills through your internal dialogue

We have thousands of thoughts a day. Our internal dialogue or thinking is the most powerful tool we have. This chapter will help you to change old and negative thinking patterns and replace them with powerful and helpful thoughts.

Internal dialogue

This is about conscious thinking and how it reinforces those beliefs that cause our emotions and actions. Our internal dialogue can cause either a vicious or a virtuous cycle of emotions and actions.

Negative automatic thoughts

These are the thoughts that appear automatically when you are in a specific situation. You will learn to first identify them and then to replace them with their more helpful versions.

Your hot thoughts

Negative, or 'hot', thoughts automatically spring up at times of intense emotion. You will be encouraged to identify your hot thoughts and helped to find their replacements so that you can immediately take control as and when they are triggered.

How to change internal dialogue

Changing internal dialogue is like changing an old habit. We need to recognize it, stop it, replace it and then repeat this, over and over again.

Past, present and future expressions

When we think about and describe ourselves, we are usually reinforcing positive or negative traits and characteristics. For example, we automatically use expressions like, 'I've always been like this', as if it is written in stone. In order to strive for our goals we need to talk about how we want to be as if we are already like that.

Constructive internal dialogue

Learning how to use constructive dialogue is about finding helpful expressions that are goal oriented. This helps to ensure we move ourselves forward by thinking in a progressive way.

Force and rigour

Our thinking needs to be forceful and passionate. You have probably seen and heard speakers who know what they are talking about and use the right words, but for some reason you end up switching off. Other speakers command attention because of the forceful and passionate way they use words.

Developing cognitive skills through your internal dialogue

So far you have been working on identifying the unhealthy beliefs that sabotage your goal achievement. You have started to develop some new cognitive skills, the 'what's in it for me' reasons, to help you focus on your goal and your new healthy beliefs.

In this chapter you will learn about the different types of thought you have and how to change them using force and rigour.

The relationship between beliefs and thoughts is shown by this modified diagram from Chapter 2.

This time the relationship is a little more elaborate. You will notice the arrows going in both directions, indicating that beliefs influence what you think, and what you think influences what you believe. Your thoughts influence your performance and your performance may trigger your thoughts. Finally, your performances and beliefs also influence each other.

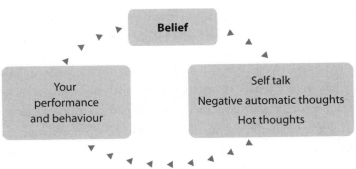

This interaction can be healthy or unhealthy, helpful or unhelpful. If your belief is healthy, the interaction between your thoughts, performance and belief is also healthy, but if your belief is unhealthy so is the interaction.

You can transform your unhealthy belief by identifying its healthy version and then taking control of your thoughts, changing them into their stronger, healthier version. So far you have learned about how to work on your belief. Now you will learn how to modify the thoughts that are influenced by the belief in order to bring about a more effective and powerful change.

You know that you develop habits or patterns through repetition. Habits can also be cognitive, in other words your thinking can become habitual through years of repetition, reinforcing the underlying beliefs that cause them in the first place.

Internal dialogue or self-talk

On any given day, thousands of thoughts go through your mind. Some of these thoughts are called 'internal dialogue' or 'self-talk'. They tend to be the things you say about yourself when you face challenges, obstacles, or problems throughout the day. Self-talk usually happens in your head at normal speed. It is just the usual dialogue you have with yourself.

All of us engage in self-talk as part of our cognitive process. What happens when your self-talk is negative and unhelpful? Years of negative, unhelpful self-talk will have an impact. If you continue to feed your mind negative self-talk, eventually you will end up developing an unhealthy belief about yourself or your abilities. This belief will in turn cause more negative self-talk. The emotional results – and your success – will be hugely influenced by this. Negative self-talk will result in a vicious cycle and become a harmful self-fulfilling prophecy. This means that as your negative self-talk is maintained, your unhealthy beliefs become stronger and your performance and emotions more badly affected. So essentially you end up thinking 'see, I knew I wouldn't be able to do it, that's typical'.

You will recognize negative self-talk from the following expressions:

- That sounds difficult
- I don't think that I can do it
- I'm sure I will mess it up
- I'm not that good
- I'll probably fail
- I've always been this way
- I give up, it's too much
- I can't believe you'd want me on your team
- I don't know much about anything
- I don't think I'm going to do a good job
- I don't think I'll impress anyone
- It's just little old me

If you fill your mind with such thoughts from the moment you wake up until you go to bed, their negativity will impact on you in a fundamental way whenever you think about yourself and your abilities.

If you hold an unhealthy belief, negative self-talk tends to be at its worst when you make a commitment to do something or when there is pressure. It is vital that you are mindful of this when you set goals and begin the process of changing unhealthy irrational beliefs.

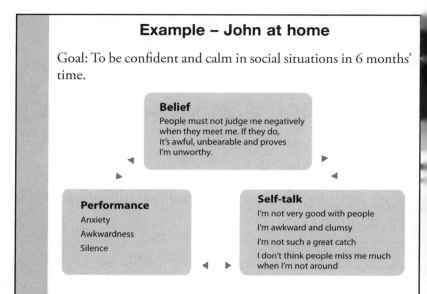

Example – John at home

Goal: To be confident and calm in social situations in 6 months' time.

Belief
People must not judge me negatively when they meet me. If they do, it's awful, unbearable and proves I'm unworthy.

Performance
Anxiety
Awkwardness
Silence

Self-talk
I'm not very good with people
I'm awkward and clumsy
I'm not such a great catch
I don't think people miss me much when I'm not around

The above diagram shows that self-talk tends to be general rather than specific. It is generated by an unhealthy demanding belief. When the belief is triggered, for example, when John agrees to go to a party, his unhealthy belief will cause other types of negative thoughts: hot thoughts and negative automatic thoughts.

What should John do?

The first thing is to identify the unhealthy and healthy beliefs as shown in Chapter 3. When the healthy belief is constructed, John will need to take control of his self-talk as well as rehearse, through repetition, his healthy belief. The change in his performance will follow through his active work on both the unhealthy belief and the self-talk it generates. You change unhealthy beliefs by attacking them from different angles.

ohn will also need to keep his 'what's in it for me' reasons at the front of his mind in order to maintain his motivation to change while feeling the natural discomfort of that change.

John's healthy belief

'd really like it if people did not judge me negatively when they meet me but that does not mean they MUST not judge me negatively either. If they do, it would be bad but not the end of the world. It would be tough but not unbearable. It would not mean I'm unworthy. I'm fallible and some people will like me and some might not. I remain worthwhile regardless because my worth does not depend on people's negative or positive judgement.

Negative automatic thoughts

Negative automatic thoughts (NAT) are the things that you always say to yourself in the same specific situations, such as going to a job interview. They are called 'automatic' because you do not take time to analyze whether they are true or not. You just accept them. They tend to be based on assumptions rather than facts. They are the product of unhealthy beliefs and, if they are not challenged, they reinforce the unhealthy belief.

It is important that you become aware of your negative automatic thoughts and the situations in which they occur, because changing them is another way for you to strengthen your healthy belief, your emotions and results. It is a good idea to identify the unhealthy beliefs that are triggered when you set a goal and the negative automatic thoughts that stem from them. Distracting yourself from them and engaging in sabotaging behaviours will not make them go away.

You will recognize negative automatic thoughts because the unhealthy belief is usually triggered. Negative automatic thoughts also tend to differ from self-talk in that you feel they come into your head faster than ordinary internal dialogue.

Example – John at a party

Goal: To be confident and calm in social situations in six months' time.

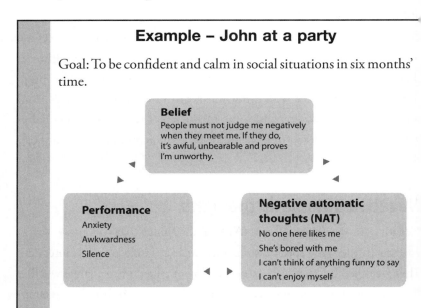

Belief
People must not judge me negatively when they meet me. If they do, it's awful, unbearable and proves I'm unworthy.

Performance
Anxiety
Awkwardness
Silence

Negative automatic thoughts (NAT)
No one here likes me
She's bored with me
I can't think of anything funny to say
I can't enjoy myself

In John's example, you have seen that his unhealthy belief triggers more specific negative thoughts. When he goes to the party, his thoughts are now specific rather than general; they feel true and more convincing.

What should John do?

John will need to bring his healthy belief to mind and start replacing his negative thoughts with positive and more helpful ones while focusing back on the party. The preparation he did at home will help him manage his thoughts more effectively while feeling the discomfort. His 'what's in it for me' reasons remind him to stay in the situation and not leave.

John's healthy belief

I'd really like it if people would not judge me negatively when they meet me but that does not mean they MUST not judge me negatively either. If they do, it would be bad but not the end of the world. It would be tough but not unbearable. It would not mean I'm unworthy. I'm fallible and some people will like me and some might not. I remain worthwhile regardless because my worth does not depend on people's negative or positive judgement.

Your hot thoughts

Hot thoughts are unhealthy beliefs that you become very conscious of, usually in times of intense emotional disturbance. Most unhealthy beliefs tend to be just beyond our conscious awareness, but when the belief is triggered, and particularly when the demand is not being met, you will experience unhealthy negative emotions such as anxiety, anger or rage very intensely. On such occasions your thoughts will be extreme, for example, awfulizing, low frustration tolerance and self- or other-damning patterns may become more pronounced. You will be more aware of thoughts like 'this is terrible', 'I can't bear this' or 'I'm so useless' or 'he's horrible'.

Example – John at the party – someone brushes him off

Goal: To be confident and calm in social situations in six months' time.

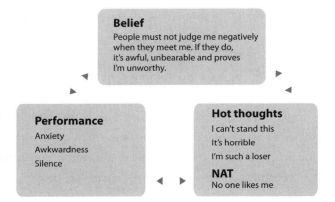

Belief
People must not judge me negatively when they meet me. If they do, it's awful, unbearable and proves I'm unworthy.

Performance
Anxiety
Awkwardness
Silence

Hot thoughts
I can't stand this
It's horrible
I'm such a loser

NAT
No one likes me

When someone at the party shrugs him off, John's thoughts become hot because his demand about being liked is not being met. This triggers his awfulizing, low frustration tolerance and self-damning beliefs. His mind is now full of these and other negative automatic thoughts.

If you imagine for a moment that John was not aware of the ABC model, unhealthy and healthy beliefs, he would have been extremely anxious and probably would have left the party.

What should John do?

John's preparation at home will give him the momentum and the awareness that he needs to challenge and weaken his unhealthy belief when someone dismisses him at the party. He will recite his healthy belief with force and rigour, challenge his hot thoughts by telling himself that they are not true or helpful to him and continue repeating his healthy belief in his head. He will stay at the party and tolerate his feelings of discomfort.

John's healthy belief

I'd really like it if people would not judge me negatively when they meet me but that does not mean they MUST not judge me negatively either. If they do, it would be bad but not the end of the world. It would be tough but not unbearable. It would not mean I'm unworthy. I'm fallible; some people will like me and some might not, but I remain worthwhile regardless because my worth does not depend on people's negative or positive judgement.

Exercise

Write down your goal, your unhealthy belief and your healthy belief, together with the 'what's in it for me' reasons.

Look at your unhealthy belief and reflect on the type of thoughts it causes.

Break these thoughts down into:

Self-Talk

Your usual internal dialogue about the problem, for example 'I'm not into going to the gym'.

Negative Automatic Thoughts

The rushed thoughts you have when you are in a situation feeling uncomfortable, for example 'exercising is so boring'.

Hot thoughts

For example, 'I can't stand being in the gym a moment longer'.

How to change internal dialogue

You already know that habits can be good, bad or neutral. First you start to think about something, then you start to repeat it and before long it becomes the way you think. It becomes normal and usual. This is the process of habit formation.

Applying the habitual process to self-talk, you will see that it is exactly the same. If you start thinking negatively and do not question the truth, sense or helpfulness of your thoughts but just keep repeating the same old nonsense then it becomes a habit. Negative self-talk is nothing more than an old bad habit. And you can change it.

The first step in any change process is to identify the problem and then set a goal. You will need to become aware of your negative self-talk by noticing how you describe yourself and your abilities, and what you say about yourself when you are faced with challenges and obstacles. If your general tendency is to say 'I give up', or 'it's too hard', your self-talk is unhelpful to you given your desire to achieve a goal.

After identifying your negative self-talk, think about a more helpful thing to say. For example, if you identify your negative self-talk as 'I give up', the more helpful thought would be 'I'll persist, I don't give up easily'.

Typical examples:

Negative Self Talk	Helpful Self Talk
That sounds difficult	It sounds challenging
I don't think that I can do it	I will have a good go
I'm sure I will mess it up	I want to do it well
I'm not that good	I'm looking forward to learning
I'll probably fail	I want to succeed
I've always been this way	I'm open to change
I give up, it's too much	I'm resilient, I don't give up easily
I can't believe you'd want me on your team	Thanks, I'm looking forward to it
I don't know much about anything	I'm eager to learn
I don't think I'm going to do a good job	I will do my very best
I don't think I'll impress anyone	I'm nervous but will go for it
It's just little old me	It's me

These examples are just some of many possible versions of helpful self-talk. Finding your own helpful expressions will make it much easier to integrate into your thinking.

It is important to remember that your helpful self-talk has to be supported by your healthy belief. If you just work on your self-talk but ignore your healthy belief, the helpful self-talk becomes more difficult to believe. For example, if you take the negative self-talk 'I'll probably fail' and the helpful self-talk 'I want to succeed', you will see that the unhealthy belief 'I must not fail because if I fail it proves I'm a failure' will sabotage your helpful self-talk. So your healthy belief about failure or success becomes 'I want to succeed but that does not mean I must and if I fail, it does not mean I am a failure. I remain worthwhile but fallible regardless'. Reciting the healthy belief will allow you to integrate the more positive self-talk of 'I want to succeed'.

Essentially you are starting the process of energizing the healthy belief by reciting it and by feeding your mind helpful self-talk while stopping the negative self-talk.

You can see the process more easily in the diagram below :

Recite healthy belief
I want to succeed but it doesn't mean I must. If I don't it doesn't mean I'm a failure. I remain worthwhile but fallible regardless.

Performance and emotions change gradually. Feelings change and after effort and consistency.

Repeat helpful self talk
I do my best
I love success
I can handle challenge or failures
My worth is inside me

How to change negative automatic thoughts

You can apply the same process to changing your negative automatic thoughts. Begin by identifying the negative automatic thoughts which are the cognitive consequence of your unhealthy belief. Write down more helpful versions that fit with the healthy belief you wish to strengthen in order to achieve your goal. Then replace the negative automatic thoughts as they come into your awareness with their helpful versions and recite your healthy belief. Repeat this process until the helpful thoughts become normal and usual.

Negative automatic thoughts tend to be present in specific situations. This means you will need to be prepared to replace them with their helpful versions there and then, and to recite your healthy belief. Becoming familiar with them in advance will make it easier for you when you are in the situation itself.

The following are some examples of negative automatic thoughts and their helpful counterparts.

Negative Automatic Thoughts	Helpful versions
No one here likes me	Some people will like me
She's bored with me	We have different interests
	I accept this possibility
I can't think of anything funny to say	I'll just be me, I'll say something funny when I'm ready
I can't enjoy myself	I will learn to enjoy myself sooner or later

These helpful versions need to be supported by the healthy belief. In John's example, the healthy belief would be:

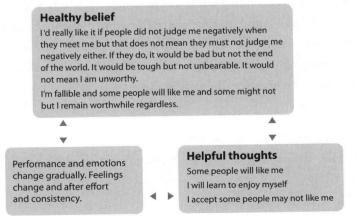

Healthy belief
I'd really like it if people did not judge me negatively when they meet me but that does not mean they must not judge me negatively either. If they do, it would be bad but not the end of the world. It would be tough but not unbearable. It would not mean I am unworthy.
I'm fallible and some people will like me and some might not but I remain worthwhile regardless.

Performance and emotions change gradually. Feelings change and after effort and consistency.

Helpful thoughts
Some people will like me
I will learn to enjoy myself
I accept some people may not like me

'I'd really like it if people would not judge me negatively when they meet me but that does not mean they must not judge me negatively either. If they do, it would be bad but not the end of the world. It would be tough but not unbearable. It would not mean I'm unworthy. I'm fallible; some people will like me and some might not, but I remain worthwhile regardless because my worth does not depend on people's negative or positive judgement.'

Helpful thoughts become more accessible if you accept the possibility of negative judgement in the first place and rid yourself of the demand that causes the negative automatic thoughts. Replacing the negative automatic thoughts as well as focusing on the healthy belief means that you are weakening the unhealthy belief from two directions.

How to change your hot thoughts

Changing your hot thoughts will yield the best and quickest results. If you are really challenged as a result of your worst scenario happening – for example failing, finding out someone thinks negatively of you, being treated unfairly – and you take control of your thoughts by changing them to their healthy versions *in that moment*, you will be taking a big step in changing your unhealthy belief. Your healthy belief will cause you to deal with the negative situation in the most helpful and constructive way.

Look back to John's example where he is brushed off by someone at a party. His hot thoughts can be replaced with healthy thoughts as follows:

Hot thoughts	Healthy versions
I can't stand this	I can stand this. It's hard but I can stand it.
It's horrible	It's not horrible. It's bad but not horrible.
I'm such a loser	I am not a loser. I'm fallible; some people will like me and some won't. I am worthy and not a loser.

Healthy thoughts can also be supported by reciting the healthy belief:

'I'd really like it if people would not judge me negatively when they meet me but that does not mean they must not judge me negatively either. If they do, it would be bad but not the end of the world. It would be tough but not unbearable. It would not mean I'm unworthy. I'm fallible; some people will like me and some might not, but I remain worthwhile regardless because my worth does not depend on people's negative or positive judgement.'

This is challenging, and John will feel intense discomfort. As he recites his healthy belief, replacing his hot thoughts with their healthy version and staying at the party, he will make a big dent in his unhealthy belief and energize his healthy belief at the same time.

Exercise

Write down your goal and healthy belief together with the 'what's in it for me' reasons.

Look at the negative examples of self-talk, negative automatic thoughts and hot thoughts you worked on in the previous exercise.

Work out their helpful and healthy versions and write them down as follows:

Helpful Self-Talk
For example, 'I'm learning to enjoy going to the gym'.

Helpful version of Negative Automatic Thoughts
If the negative automatic thought was 'exercising is so boring', the helpful thought could be 'exercising is challenging at the moment but good for my goal'.

Healthy version of Hot Thoughts
If the hot thought is 'I can't stand being in the gym for a moment longer', the healthy version would be 'I can definitely stand being in the gym for another half an hour even though it's challenging at the moment'.

Start rehearsing and repeating the healthy versions each time the negative or unhelpful thoughts come into your mind.

Support your helpful thinking by reciting your healthy beliefs when you are challenged.

Past, present and future expressions

Remember that when you describe yourself, you reinforce positive or negative traits and characteristics. For example, you may automatically say, 'I've always been like this'. In striving for your goals, you need to bring the present and what you are currently doing into your self-talk.

You are usually unaware of how your internal dialogue or self-talk reinforces your healthy or unhealthy beliefs, attitudes and traits. You may carelessly use expressions like, 'yes, that's so me' when you have forgotten something, or you may say, 'I'm always late'. You are allowing these thoughts to continue filtering through your mind, shaping how you think of yourself. If you decide that you want to make a change and achieve your goal, it is important to acknowledge that you are *now* striving for change and to be mindful of expressions that describe you as you were in the past, with your old habits and attitudes.

Essentially, your self-talk decides that you 'are' or 'are not' a particular way. If you say 'I find going to the gym boring' then you are confirming and reinforcing a past trait – you are not 'someone who likes the gym'. You may think, 'but that's how I feel about it'. The truth of the matter is that's how you have felt about it up to now. There is a possibility that you may change that thinking if you are open to it, and particularly if you have an important goal to achieve. Expressions based on past conditioning do not take your goal into consideration. If you have a goal to lose weight and going to the gym is one of your weight loss strategies, telling yourself that you are someone who doesn't like the gym will affect your motivation. All you are doing is affirming old thinking, bringing the past into the present and into your future. Instead, you can bring your goal, choice and desires into your mind when you are thinking about the gym.

Changing your self-talk expressions gives you a simple and truthful way of talking about the present. You don't have to lie by telling yourself that you love going to the gym. That would be too far removed from the current truth. But you can say, 'I am choosing to go the gym and hopefully will learn to enjoy it because I have a goal to achieve'. This new self-talk is a more accurate reflection of what you are now doing and wanting to achieve.

Constructive internal dialogue

Constructive internal dialogue means talking to yourself in a way that helps you keep unhelpful traits and characteristics firmly in the past because they hinder your goal. It's about reinforcing your successful traits and characteristics.

If you have traits and habits that hinder your goal, then express them in the past tense and reiterate the present and future desire. For example, you could say 'I used to be someone who found the gym boring, but now I'm hoping to enjoy it at some point because I have a goal to achieve'. This new expression is a more accurate description of your present reality.

It is equally important to affirm your success and the fact that you are now challenging old traits and behaviours. This is about taking responsibility and acknowledging the helpful changes you are now making. Instead of criticizing yourself, you can give yourself a pat on the back and congratulate yourself on your success or hard work.

You have now learned a way of talking and thinking that is grounded in resiliency and high tolerance of discomfort when you are challenging yourself.

Examples

I used to be someone who hated getting up early; now I choose to get up early to have more time because I want to achieve my goal. In time, getting up early will be easier.

I used to be someone who always said yes; now I'm learning to be more assertive so I'm learning to say no.

I used to be someone who found socializing very hard; now I'm learning to stretch my comfort zone and hopefully I will learn to enjoy it.

I used to be someone who got very anxious; now I'm learning new ways to deal with my feelings and eventually I will feel calm.

I used to be someone who procrastinated a lot; now I'm learning how to beat that habit because I want to be more productive.

Exercise

Write your goal and healthy beliefs down, for example:

Goal: To be confident in social situations in six months' time.

Healthy belief: I'd really like people to like me but they don't have to. If they don't, it doesn't mean I'm a failure. I'm worthy but fallible.

Reflect on the self-talk expressions about your traits and habits that are unhelpful to your goal because they fixate you on the past. Write these expressions down, for example, 'I'm always shy in social situations'.

Use the above examples to express your constructive thoughts more truthfully so they can support your goal. For example: 'I used to be shy in social situations. Now I'm learning to be confident by working on my healthy belief.'

Force and vigour

Your thinking needs to be forceful and passionate, like that of those teachers who are very effective at lecturing or presenting and engage your attention and interest. Positively persuasive and memorable teachers are skilled at the following:

- explaining their subject
- enabling students to personalize the information
- helping students understand the benefits of what they are learning
- capturing the attention of their students.

One of the main reasons their subjects appear more interesting and lively is that the information is communicated in a forceful, passionate, energetic and lively manner. Passion and energy help the message to be communicated well, enabling it to sink in and become integrated into the listener's psyche. The same applies when you want to replace your old unhealthy beliefs with the healthy ones.

Healthy beliefs integrate into the psyche more effectively if you rehearse and recite them with force and energy, as opposed to in a lacklustre, half-hearted manner. This way you will believe the healthy beliefs quicker. When this happens your emotions will change accordingly.

You can see how this also applies to your

- self-talk,
- helpful thoughts and
- healthy thoughts.

Think about what happens if you recite your healthy belief in a half-hearted way. For example, read the following in a low, weak voice:

'I am a worthwhile, valuable but fallible person.'

They are just words and reading them in this way conveys no feeling in your body.

Passion, forcefulness and the energy you put behind your words matter when you are trying to trigger an emotional response. Now read the same words, putting all these elements into your voice as you read them:

'I AM A WORTHWHILE, VALUABLE BUT FALLIBLE PERSON.'

You are in the process of changing a habit. This may feel odd at first, but with repetition you will get used to it provided you already know in your head that it is a true, logical and helpful statement. Remember that your feelings will change last. If you did not feel odd at reading it with energy and passion, you will have noticed a stronger positive emotion in your body.

Forceful healthy beliefs

When you recite and rehearse your healthy beliefs, self-talk, helpful thoughts and healthy thoughts it's important that you inject as much passion and energy into them as is appropriate for you. In particular, you need to do this when you are negating the most disturbing beliefs.

Emphasize the want but then emphasize the anti-demand more:

I want xyz but I DON'T HAVE TO HAVE IT.

When you are reciting the anti-catastrophizing belief, emphasize that it is not the end of the world:

If I don't get what I want, it will be bad BUT IT WON'T BE THE END OF THE WORLD.

When you are rehearsing your high frustration tolerance belief, emphasize that you are tolerating it, bearing it, or able to stand it for longer:

If I don't get what I want, it would be tough BUT I CAN STAND AND TOLERATE IT.

And finally, when you are rehearsing your self-acceptance belief, empha-size the whole belief:

If I don't get what I want, IT DOES NOT MEAN I AM WORTHLESS. I AM WORTHWHILE BUT FALLIBLE, REGARDLESS.

Forceful and constructive self-talk or internal dialogue

As mentioned earlier, forcefulness and energy also need to be applied to your constructive self-talk. Here, the emphasis needs to be on what you were like in the past and what you are now doing in the present.

Use force and passion to convince yourself that the trait or attitude you are changing belongs firmly to the past. Then energetically emphasize what you are doing now. For example:

I USED TO BE someone who always said yes, NOW I'M LEARNING TO BE MORE ASSERTIVE. I'M LEARNING TO SAY NO.

Forceful helpful thoughts

Helpful thoughts are the counterparts to automatic negative thoughts which occur in the specific situation that triggers the belief. In such situ-ations you will have a very good opportunity not only to recite your healthy belief in a forceful manner but also to replace your automatic negative thoughts with helpful ones.

When you replace your negative automatic thoughts with helpful versions, you will need to emphasize the positive, your acceptance of yourself and acceptance of what's not within your control. For example:

Some people WILL like me.
I WILL learn to enjoy myself.
I ACCEPT some people may not like me.

The idea is to be forceful about the specific aspect of the thought that is most challenging, in order to integrate the new thoughts into your belief system more effectively.

Forceful, healthy thoughts

Forceful, healthy thoughts are counterparts to hot thoughts, which you experience during intense emotional experiences and when your demand is not being met. They are the healthy version of the hot thoughts.

In such a situation, remember that you may need to be more forceful and emphatic about the anti-catastrophizing thoughts than the high frustration tolerance ones, simply because the hot thoughts are more about catastrophizing. Alternatively, you may need to emphasize other healthy thoughts depending on the theme of the hot thought you are experiencing. For example:

I CAN stand this. It's hard BUT I CAN stand it.
IT'S NOT horrible. It's bad BUT NOT horrible.
I am NOT a loser. I'M FALLIBLE so some people will like me and some won't.
I AM WORTHY and NOT a loser.

Exercise

Start rehearsing and reciting your healthy beliefs, self-talk, helpful thoughts and healthy thoughts in a forceful and energetic manner at least twice a day and each time the old thoughts creep in.

CHAPTER 6

Using imagination and visualization

For most of us, the first place to start the process of goal achievement is in the mind. This chapter is about using your imagination and internal dialogue, seeing yourself actively engaged in your actions and concentrating on the end results.

Start with your imagination

Your mind reacts to images and thoughts. The more you imagine yourself doing something in a vivid and emotive way, the more your mind accepts that you can actually do it.

Internal dialogue

Imagining yourself striving and achieving in order to reach your goals needs to be combined with constructive thinking. There is little point in taking the time to imagine yourself positively yet think in a negative way for the rest of the day.

Future image

What you imagine needs to be future-based. This means you need to imagine yourself as you want to be before it becomes a reality for you.

Repetition

Remember that repetition is key. The more you repeat the more you reinforce a belief or habit.

Using imagination and visualization

So far, you have learned to identify the unhealthy beliefs that cause your negative emotions, behaviours and thoughts, and to construct their healthy counterparts. Your healthy beliefs are the foundation of your goal and its achievement. You've also learned to think about your 'what's in it for me' reasons. These enable you to remain motivated to focus on your goal as you go through the natural state of discomfort and tension caused by change.

You have learned that, in order to change your unhealthy belief, you need to focus on your goal, stop the unhealthy negative thoughts, replace them with their healthy versions, and then behave in accordance with your healthy belief while tolerating the state of discomfort. This discomfort is natural and, to make it more acceptable, can be reframed as natural excitement. You have also learned to remain focused on your goal as you work to overcome the obstacles that come up.

In this chapter, you will learn different techniques so you can use your imagination, coupled with powerful self-talk, in a vivid and emotive way. Doing this will strengthen your healthy belief when you combine it with your constructive self-talk.

As you start your move towards your goal, you may find that acting in accordance with your healthy belief is overwhelming. It helps to plan and prepare before taking action. Even if you do not find making a change too overwhelming, a great way of engaging your mind in a powerful way is to aim for success but be smart and plan for the worst-case scenario. This means that you can respond to such an eventuality in a more appropriate and psychologically helpful manner.

This does not mean responding to bad events with a smile and a skip, but experiencing the healthy negative emotions appropriately and then moving on. This is at the core of cognitive behaviour therapy. It is about viewing the glass as half full, but learning to deal with life when the glass is in fact half empty without damaging yourself, so you can eventually see it as being half full again.

In the last chapter, you learned about the importance of force and vigour in the way you recite and rehearse your healthy belief and in how you use your self-talk and helpful and healthy thoughts. Now you will learn about using your imagination in a vivid way. A powerful imagination is another tool in the resources that enable you to make a change in your beliefs.

Think back to when you experienced a negative event in the past and found yourself stuck. How did you talk to yourself and engage your imagination? It's likely that you were passionate and energetic in talking to yourself negatively. Your imagination was probably powerful and full of emotions. Is it any wonder you felt stuck?

If you think how this process can be reversed, using your healthy beliefs and focusing on your goal, you can see that you are using passionate intensity and vivid imagination in a different way, for your own good rather than for your own sabotage. If you have the ability to sabotage yourself well and truly then you have the capability of freeing yourself from unhealthy old beliefs. Just take control, challenge your unhealthy beliefs, make a commitment to your **SMART** goal, use your mind and take appropriate action. And of course you need to repeat it in a consistent manner over and over again.

Start with your imagination

There are many ways of using your imagination to strengthen healthy beliefs and weaken unhealthy beliefs. It is more effective to imagine the negative or worst-case scenario first before you move on to positive thinking.

A healthy belief cannot be strengthened without first imagining yourself dealing with the 'not getting what you want' in a healthy way and rating yourself negatively.

Imagining a healthy response to a negative event – healthy belief

Your first task is to vividly imagine yourself responding healthily to not getting what you want.

1. Write down your goal and healthy belief.
2. Sit or lie down.
3. Close your eyes.
4. Breathe in deeply, hold it for three or four seconds and then breathe out gently. Repeat a couple of times.
5. Imagine a scenario or a scene where your healthy desire is not being met. Imagine this as strongly as you can for maximum emotional discomfort. *If you are imagining the worst-case scenario then you will feel discomfort. This is natural. It means you have hit the target of your fear.*

6. While imagining the worst-case scenario, start reciting your healthy belief forcefully and energetically.

7. Continue to imagine the negative event and recite your healthy belief until you notice a positive change to your emotions.

8. Open your eyes.

Example – John using the imagination technique at home

Goal: To be confident and calm in social situations in six months' time.

John's healthy belief

I'd really like it if people would not judge me negatively when they meet me but that does not mean they MUST not judge me negatively either. If they do, it would be bad but not the end of the world. It would be tough but not unbearable. It would not mean I'm unworthy. I'm fallible; some people will like me and some might not, but I remain worthwhile regardless because my worth does not depend on people's negative or positive judgement.

John sits down and closes his eyes.

He begins to breathe in deeply and exhale slowly.

He then visualizes a scenario in which someone is clearly judging him negatively. He concentrates on his worst-case scenario where someone dismisses him and calls him dull. John fully and vividly imagines this negative event by adding other people who hear the remark. As John imagines this he begins to feel very uncomfortable emotionally.

When his feelings of discomfort peak he begins to recite his healthy belief as follows:

I'd really like it if people would not judge me negatively when they meet me but that *does not mean they must not judge me negatively either.* If they do, it would be bad *but not the end of the world.* It would be tough but *not unbearable. It would not mean I'm unworthy. I'm fallible*; and some people will like me and some might not, but *I remain worthwhile* regardless because my worth *does not depend on people's negative or positive judgement.*

He recites his healthy belief energetically and forcefully, emphasizing the aspects he wants to strengthen.

He continues to recite his healthy belief while imagining the negative event until his feelings are no longer uncomfortable.

He opens his eyes.

What if the feeling of discomfort is overwhelming?

When you imagine the worst-case scenario you may find the feelings of discomfort so overwhelming that you stop the imagining technique. This only means that the unhealthy belief is very strong, and that it is interrupting your ability to visualize because it is causing such strong emotions. There is a way around this, called the bridging technique, which involves borrowing a more positive feeling from another memory so that you can continue with your initial visualization.

According to the laws of psychology, a stronger emotion can override another and anxiety is incompatible with thirst, hunger, sexual arousal or relaxation. This means that, for example, you cannot be hungry and anxious at the same time, or anxious and thirsty or sexually aroused and anxious at the same time. The easiest way to understand this is to remember that anxiety is an emotion we feel when there is danger or threat. So if you imagine yourself sitting down eating a sandwich and then see that a lion is staring at you, thinking, 'mmmm … lunch', you won't feel like finishing your sandwich before you run.

If you find that imagining the negative event triggers overwhelming feelings of discomfort, you can use this insight to your advantage. The purpose is to desensitize yourself a little to the imagined negative event. In effect, you are increasing your tolerance to the discomfort by making yourself feel more relaxed or more positive before you begin.

Essentially you are 'borrowing' the feeling of relaxation or positivity from another memory, forming a bridge from one image to another. The positive feelings will mix with the feelings of discomfort attached to the negative image you are imagining.

Triggering a positive feeling and imagining a healthy response to a negative event – healthy belief

1. Write down your goal and healthy belief.
2. Sit or lie down.
3. Close your eyes.
4. Breathe in deeply, hold it for three or four seconds and then breathe out gently. Repeat a couple of times.
5. In your mind, recall a time when you felt very relaxed, or when you had strong positive feelings.
6. Focus on the memory and recall where you were and what was happening.
7. Imagine that memory as if it is happening to you right now.
8. Be aware of the increasing feelings of relaxation or positivity.
9. Imagine these feelings growing stronger.
10. When you are ready, let your mind go blank.

11. Imagine a scenario where your healthy desire is not being met. Imagine this vividly for maximum emotional discomfort. *If you are imagining the worst-case scenario then you will feel discomfort. This is natural. It means you have hit the target of your fear.*

12. While imagining the worst-case scenario, start reciting your healthy belief forcefully and energetically.

13. Continue to imagine the negative event and recite your healthy belief until you notice a positive change in your emotions.

14. Open your eyes.

Practise these techniques daily until your discomfort feels more appropriate and manageable. It is important to do them regularly and they will only take a few minutes. You can go over them at home, on the bus or train, or during your lunch break. The important thing is that you show commitment to achieving your goal by putting in the effort to change your unhealthy beliefs.

Using audio

When it comes to making the process of changing your beliefs varied and interesting, the only limitation is how easy you find it to use your imagination. You may find that visualization doesn't work well for you. Some people have strong visual ability and others find it difficult. If visualization techniques are not your cup of tea, then you can record your healthy beliefs, thoughts and 'what's in it for me' reasons and listen to them instead.

It is very important that you record your healthy beliefs and thoughts in a forceful and energetic manner. The more passion you inject into your recording the more effective you will be at integrating and believing them.

The point here is to make your rehearsal techniques, whether they are imagined or auditory, as memorable and as vivid as possible. This way you will engage your emotions, and the more emotive you make your cognitive techniques the better.

Rehearsing your belief and your 'what's in it for me' reasons – auditory

This technique involves listening to your recording of your healthy belief and your personal 'what's in it for me' motivation, and the reasons why you no longer want the unhealthy version. You are literally hearing yourself saying, 'I want this healthy belief and not that old one'.

You can make your recording in any way that works for you, for example using a digital recording device, a tape recorder or your PC.

What do you do?

1. Write down your goal and healthy beliefs.
2. Write down the 'what's in it for me' reasons that support your healthy belief.
3. Write down your unhealthy belief and the 'what's in it for me' reasons for this belief. These are all the negative things it causes.
4. Record your healthy belief in a forceful, energetic manner, as follows:

    I choose my healthy belief of (insert your healthy belief). I choose it because I (or it) will (insert your 'what's in it for me' reasons).

    I have no desire for the old unhealthy belief that said (insert your unhealthy belief). I have no desire for it because it causes me (insert your 'what's in it for me' reasons for the unhealthy belief). (Record these reasons as if you are tired and annoyed with your unhealthy belief.)

I choose my healthy belief that says (insert your healthy belief). (Record this in a tone that affirms your choice of your healthy belief.)

5. End of recording.

Remember to make your recording forceful, energetic and passionate by varying the tone, speed and volume of your voice.

Making the recording should only take a few minutes and you can listen to it whenever you want. Repeating it three or four more times can work very well.

You can listen to your recording while walking to work, or when you are in your car, on the train or the bus.

Example – John's audio recording

Goal: To be confident and calm in social situations in six months' time.

- I choose my healthy belief. I'd really like it if people would not judge me negatively when they meet me but that does not mean they must not judge me negatively either. If they do, it would be bad but not the end of the world. It would be tough but not unbearable. It would not mean I'm unworthy. I'm fallible; some people will like me and some might not, but I remain worthwhile regardless because my worth does not depend on people's negative or positive judgement.

- I choose it because I will feel more relaxed and not anxious. I will be me. I will enjoy myself more. I will allow people to know me. People will probably like me because I'm being me. I will feel strong and cope if someone does not like me. I will express what I think and feel better. I will agree when I agree with someone. I will disagree when I disagree with someone. I will be focused on the conversation and on the people I'm talking to. I will get a better sense of other people because I won't be in my head all the time. My hands will be fine. I will be cool and comfortable. I will feel that I have a right just like everyone else. I will like myself. I will be open and happy. I will feel more confident in myself. I will have good conversations and be able to chat up someone I fancy. I will be relaxed and laugh and joke freely. I will be great.

- I have no desire for the old belief that people must not judge me negatively when they meet me and if they do, it's awful, unbearable and proves I'm unworthy. I have no desire for it because it makes me feel anxious and not myself in the company of other people. I have no desire for it because it makes me worry about what to say and how I'm saying things. It stops me from engaging. It makes me focused on my feelings and not on the conversation. It makes my hands shake. It makes me sweat and go red. It makes me feel like I'm clumsy. It makes me run out of things to say. It makes me agree with everything people say even if I disagree in my head. It makes me end up talking to people I don't want to talk to. It makes me decline invitations and it affects my social life.

- I choose my healthy belief that I'd really like it if people would not judge me negatively when they meet me but that does not mean they must not judge me negatively either. If they do, it would be bad but not the end of the world. It would be tough but not unbearable. It would not mean I'm unworthy. I'm fallible; some people will like me and some might not, but I remain worthwhile regardless because my worth does not depend on people's negative or positive judgement.

Other audio recordings

In Chapter 5 you learned how to put together constructive self-talk, and helpful and healthy thoughts. These can also be recorded in a forceful way, using the following step-by-step easy guide.

1. Write down your goal and healthy belief.
2. Write down your healthy self-talk expressions.
3. Write down your helpful thoughts.
4. Write down your healthy thoughts.
5. Record your healthy belief, in a forceful manner, as follows:
   * I choose to ensure that my self-talk is powerful and helpful. This is how I speak to myself now (insert your helpful self-talk expressions).
   * I choose to think in a way that helps when I'm in specific situations. This is how I now think when I'm challenged (insert your helpful thoughts).
   * I choose to forcefully replace any negative thoughts when things do not go my way in specific situations. I now say (insert healthy thoughts).
   * I choose my healthy belief (insert healthy belief).
6. End recording.

Example – John's other audio recording

Goal: To be confident and calm in social situations in six months' time.

- I'd really like it if people would not judge me negatively when they meet me but that does not mean they must not judge me negatively either. If they do, it would be bad but not the end of the world. It would be tough but not unbearable. It would not mean I'm unworthy. I'm fallible; some people will like me and some might not, but I remain worthwhile regardless because my worth does not depend on people's negative or positive judgement.

- I choose to ensure that my self-talk is powerful and helpful. This is how I speak to myself now. I used to be someone who always said yes, now I'm learning to be more assertive. I'm learning to say no. I used to be someone who found socializing very hard, now I'm learning to stretch my comfort zone and hopefully I will learn to enjoy it.

- I choose to think in a way that helps when I'm in specific situations. This is how I now think when I'm challenged: 'Some people will like me'; 'We have different interests'; 'I accept this possibility'; 'I'll just be me'; 'I'll say something funny when I'm ready'; 'I will learn to enjoy myself sooner or later'.

- I choose to forcefully replace any negative thoughts when things do not go my way in specific situations. I now say: 'I can stand this'; 'It's just hard but I can stand it'; 'It's not horrible'; 'It's bad but not horrible'; 'I am not a loser'; 'I'm fallible, some people will like me and some won't'; 'I am worthy and not a loser'.

- I choose my healthy belief. I'd really like it if people would not judge me negatively when they meet me but that does not mean they must not judge me negatively either. If they do, it would be bad but not the end of the world. It would be tough but not unbearable. It would not mean I'm unworthy. I'm fallible; some people will like me and some might not, but I remain worthwhile regardless because my worth does not depend on people's negative or positive judgement.

If you like, you can enhance the imagining techniques by first practising them and then listening to the recording.

You can also record instructions for your imagining techniques, then close your eyes and listen to your self-instructions.

You can record instructions for relaxation followed by instructions for the imagining technique, then the audio affirmations and forceful statements. There are many variations – be creative and enjoy creating your own combinations.

The following is a step-by-step guide:

1. Write down your goal and healthy belief.
2. Write down your helpful and constructive self-talk expressions.
3. Write down your helpful thoughts.
4. Write down your healthy thoughts.

5. Record the following:
   - Sit or lie down.
   - Close your eyes now.
   - Breathe in deeply, hold it for three or four seconds and then breathe out slowly and gently.
   - Repeat the breathing exercise five or six times.
   - Recall a time when you felt really relaxed. (Pause for a while.)
   - Now focus on the memory. Recall where you were and what was happening. (Pause for a while.)
   - Imagine yourself in that memory as if it is happening to you right now. Notice the feeling of relaxation. (Pause for a while.)
   - Be aware of the increasing feelings of relaxation. (Pause for a while.)
   - Imagine these feelings growing stronger. (Pause for a while.)
   - Let your mind go blank.
   - Imagine a scenario where your healthy desire is not being met. Imagine this vividly. As soon as you feel uncomfortable recite your healthy belief. (Pause for a while.)
   - Keep reciting your healthy belief more forcefully. (Pause for a while.)
   - Keep reciting your healthy belief until you notice a change in your feelings.
   - Tell yourself that you will ensure your self-talk is powerful and constructive from now on. (Pause for a while.)
   - Repeat your powerful self-talk expressions. (Pause for a while.)
   - Tell yourself that you choose to think in a helpful way in specific situations when you are challenged. (Pause for a while.)
   - Recite your helpful thoughts. (Pause for a while.)
   - Tell yourself that you choose to forcefully replace your negative thoughts when things do not go your way. (Pause for a while.)

- Recite your healthy thoughts. (Pause for a while.)
- Recite your healthy belief one last time.
- Open your eyes.

You can of course open your eyes and read what you have written, and then close your eyes and continue listening to your own instructions. Just read, shut your eyes and begin to imagine vividly.

Positive imagery after you have imagined dealing with the negative

So far, the techniques that you have learned are about facing up to the worst-case scenario. This is at the core of changing your unhealthy beliefs. However, once you notice that your feelings are changing – i.e. you are no longer 'dreading' the negative event – you can move on to positive thinking. Remember to work on the negative event first before you start working towards positive thinking.

Positive thinking means that you start imagining your goal has been achieved. Your goal is about your desire but it needs to be supported by your healthy, realistic belief. Your healthy belief is focused on your desire but it allows for the external possibility that sometimes you may not get what you want. So far you have learned how to use imagining techniques that strengthen your healthy response to this external possibility. Now you can imagine that you have achieved your desire and goal.

Two futures – positive imagining technique

This technique involves imagining yourself dealing with not getting what you want in a powerful and healthy way and then imagining yourself getting what you want. These two images are both supported by your healthy belief.

1. Write down your goal and healthy belief.
2. Sit or lie down.
3. Close your eyes.
4. Breathe in deeply and hold it for three or four seconds and then breathe out gently. Repeat this five or six times.
5. Recite your healthy belief in a forceful and energetic manner. You can do this either silently or out loud.
6. Imagine the negative event of your healthy belief but imagine yourself responding in a healthy and helpful manner.
7. Recite your healthy belief again.
8. Imagine your goal achieved.
9. Open your eyes.

You can add other techniques, for example, you can start with the relaxation or positive feelings technique. You can also record the instructions for this technique, then just lie down, listen and participate in your imagination.

Internal dialogue

You have already learned about the significance of your self-talk or internal dialogue. Imagining yourself striving and achieving your goal needs to be combined with constructive and helpful thinking. There is little point in taking time to imagine yourself dealing with the negative event and imagining yourself with your goal achieved if you revert to old ways of thinking for the rest of the day.

Sometimes it's very easy to read about different techniques and then to forget about them. It's important to put what you are reading into practice, otherwise all you will have is knowledge and insight without a change in your emotions. It is important that you take control of your self-talk and change it to ensure it is constructive and helpful to you.

Your self-talk needs to help you to remain open-minded, creative and focused on your goal.

Be aware that you will feel some discomfort when you make the effort to practise your imagining techniques. This is natural. Take care to ensure that your internal dialogue reflects this natural state and make it positive, hopeful and constructive.

You have already planned your helpful self-talk expressions relating to your belief. Remember that changing self-talk is like changing an old habit and you will need to:

- Understand the problem of negative self-talk.
- Understand what the positive, powerful and constructive self-talk is all about.
- Make a commitment to yourself to change the old negative self-talk habit.
- Remind yourself of this goal daily.
- Stop the negative self-talk and immediately change it to its helpful and positive version.

If you follow these steps you will become very aware of your self-talk and become more and more proficient at changing it.

How do you remind yourself of your commitment to your positive and constructive self-talk?

There are many ways of reminding yourself of your commitment to healthier self-talk. One is to write down your commitment in the form of an affirmation, in other words a statement of your new position on something, or how you want to be in the future, as if it has already happened.

Structuring an affirmation

An affirmation describes how you wish to be with a positive benefit, written as if it has already happened. The following guidelines will help you to write your affirmation:

- *Use first person*: 'I'.
- *Use present tense*: 'I am' instead of 'I will'.
- *Be positive*: 'I am calm because my self-talk is constructive' instead of 'I am not anxious because my self talk is constructive'.
- *Be realistic*: don't use the words 'always' or 'never'.
- *Make it emotive*: use powerful words that trigger positive emotions for you, for example, 'I am achieving because my self talk is powerful and helpful'.

Reflective exercise

As with most things in life, your affirmation about your self-talk needs to include something that will motivate you, in the same way as your 'what's in it for me' reasons. Think about why positive and powerful self-talk is of benefit to you. Would it help you to feel more confident? Would it encourage you to become more goal striving? Would it help you to take more risks and feel less fearful? What would it do for you?

Take a couple of minutes to write down your answers to the above questions.

Write your own self-talk affirmation using the guidelines above.

How to use your self-talk affirmation

Once you have written your self-talk affirmation (for example, 'I feel confident because my self talk is positive and helpful'), the next step is to start repeating it mentally, as often as you can, every day. You have learned about reciting your healthy beliefs and helpful and healthy thoughts forcefully and energetically. You've learned about the value of vivid imagining in integrating the healthy belief. The same rules apply to affirmations about your self-talk.

Rehearsing your self-talk affirmation needs to be forceful, energetic and, where possible, vivid. For example, you can write your affirmation and save it as a computer screen saver so it flashes in front of you as you work. You can write it on a big sheet of coloured paper and have it next to your bed so that you see it immediately when you wake up. You can stick it on your fridge so that you see another vivid reminder every time you open it. In your car, you can stick it on the mirror or on the dashboard.

You can also use metaphoric imagery to remind yourself of your self-talk commitment. For example, you might imagine yourself in a gym practising pull-ups over a bar and on that bar are the words 'self-talk' – you could use such words as powerful or uplifting or strong. This is a really useful, vivid and highly emotive way of working.

Read the following affirmation:

I find it easy to keep my internal dialogue positive and helpful.

Take a moment and think about the metaphoric image it conjures up in your mind.

Bring this image to mind each time you recite and rehearse your self-talk, helping to integrate your new way of thinking. Your self-talk influ-

:nces and reinforces your belief and performance so it is important for
/ou to take control of it and make it work for the benefit of your goal.

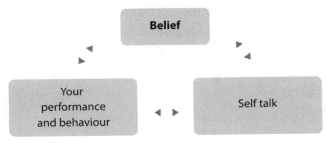

Future image

All of your constructive imagery work on integrating healthy beliefs is
future-based, meaning that you are imagining it as if it has already happened. This helps you to shift to your new belief about what you can do
– provided, of course, you have already identified your unhealthy belief
and accepted the notion that the possibility of not getting what you
want exists, i.e. you are working in accordance with your healthy belief.

When you begin to imagine yourself doing something proactive and
constructive, sooner or later you will begin to accept that you can in fact
do it. So imagining yourself as you want to be as if it has already happened strengthens your belief in your own abilities. You will begin to
allow for the possibility that you can do it. You will start to feel a sense
of motivation and eagerness to get on with it. Remember that as obstacles are identified, you work to overcome them without compromising
your healthy goal. This means you continue to imagine yourself with
your goal achieved as you deal with the obstacles in an appropriate way.

Once you begin to integrate the possibility that you can do something
which previously felt too overwhelming, and once your self-talk is con-

gruent with this, you can reach a plateau. This means you now believe that you can do what you want to do. You are acknowledging your potential. If you are at this stage but still finding it difficult to put your plan into action, you can step up a gear in your cognitive skills and start thinking and talking to yourself as if you have achieved your goal. This means you are now talking in accordance with your goal-achieving self. Start using expressions that demonstrate your commitment rather than your potential.

For example:

- 'I am working towards my goal.'
- 'I am dealing with challenges and obstacles.'
- 'I am overcoming my fears.'
- 'In the past I used expressions like "I can"; now I say "I am".'

So at this stage you stop the self-talk expressions that are based on your potential 'I can' or 'I will at some point'. This is simply because you are now beyond that point. You now know that you have the potential, and your thoughts need to generate and trigger the natural feeling of discomfort and excitement of commitment. As you know, in order to drive faster, you shift a gear. This is your shift in gear, cognitively speaking.

Repetition

Repetition is one of the significant parts of the change process. Do it again and again and again and again. All your usual, automatic ways of operating have become like that simply because you have repeated them.

Your unhealthy beliefs and negative self-images only became believable because you entertained them in your mind and thought about them with force and passion. You repeated them energetically. You imagined them vividly.

To shift to the healthy side and to strengthen your healthy beliefs, to change your self-talk, to move towards your goal, requires you to repeat them in a forceful, energetic and vivid way. You were an expert at doing that on the unhealthy, negative side. You know that all you have to do is apply the same degree of commitment and repetition to your goal and healthy beliefs. In time you will experience a shift in your beliefs and self-image.

Everything in your life that you are confident about has gone through the same process. You repeated constructive thoughts and imagined powerful, positive and strong images about yourself. Emotive repetition has been at the core of it all.

You know you have repeated the negative and the positive in the past, not just once or twice but many, many times. You have been like a passionate broken record. Now you need to apply the same passion to your new beliefs, your thoughts and your goals. You can keep these concepts and beliefs alive by imagining them, rehearsing them and talking about them to yourself. Make sure you repeat them by using diagrams, stickers, audio machines and anything that helps trigger your memory. By committing to the repetition, you will be making a commitment to yourself.

CHAPTER 7

Developing resiliency

This chapter will help you learn how to tolerate challenges and draw upon the vast supply of resources you already have. It will remind you to use the cognitive techniques you've learned so far, and introduce you to disputing skills to reinforce resiliency.

Challenges

You will learn how to see challenges as a temporary part of the goal achievement process.

Resources for resiliency and how to access them cognitively

All your positive experiences are stored in your mind. To help you develop resiliency, you can access them together with their associated feelings. In other words, you can learn how to 'borrow' positive feelings attached to memories from your past and use them in the here and now.

Cognitive disputing skills

These skills are vital in helping you question your thinking pattern as you learn to develop resiliency. Disputing skills include asking yourself the questions: 1) is it realistic, 2) does it make sense, and 3) does it help me?

Develop resiliency

So far you have learned about CBT processes and how to apply them to achieve your goals. At the core of your emotional challenges are your beliefs. Your healthy beliefs are the foundation on which your goal is built and your unhealthy beliefs are at the core of your emotional disturbance and goal sabotage. You've learned that in order to shift and change your beliefs you need to tolerate the discomfort of change. Re-naming these feelings as natural discomfort and excitement may help you accept this state more easily and so not give up. Effectively, you are putting a positive spin on this feeling of discomfort.

While you are tolerating this natural state of discomfort, You also need to keep focusing on your goal and deal with any challenges that spring up along the way. You can do this by changing your unhealthy beliefs and the different types of thought they cause, replacing them with their healthy versions. You know that one of the things you can be sure of in this whole process is feeling and experiencing the discomfort and challenge of change. Using the cognitive skills you have learned so far, you can develop resiliency to help you bounce back from any setbacks while learning from the challenges they present.

Your mind is a reservoir of experiences, memories, learning and resources that you can put to good use to help you tolerate your emotions and remain focused on your goal. You will learn a specific, structured approach to thinking called 'disputing' to help you respond to challenges and strengthen your resiliency. You can use disputing skills whenever you experience emotional challenges.

Challenges

You may experience a number of challenges when you want to achieve something. Some are within your control and some are not. Whether or not these experiences are within your control, it will always come down to how you are feeling about them.

Within your control
Your own beliefs

On the whole your beliefs, healthy or unhealthy, are now up to you. Everyone is shaped by their upbringing, how they are nurtured and the influence of people in their lives when growing up. As a child, you may have been persuaded into your beliefs but this does not mean you are stuck with them forever, especially if they are causing you problems now. You can change them.

Even if someone has been well nurtured, this is no guarantee that they will grow up with healthy beliefs. Everyone has unhealthy beliefs. As an adult, you are responsible for how you wish to live. If you wish to live in accordance with unhelpful beliefs about yourself, your past, your parents, the world, then you need to accept that you will live unhappily. Your unhealthy beliefs will be causing your emotions, behaviour, thoughts and symptoms. You may not have had a choice as a child but now you can make a better choice for yourself. It may not be easy but it is possible to change your unhealthy beliefs and learn to live more happily.

These beliefs may be about:

- love
- rejection
- failure
- making mistakes
- being perfect
- talking in public
- blushing
- confrontation
- being thin or fat, tall or short
- getting on a train, plane or car
- being on your own
- getting married
- having children
- death
- loss
- acceptance
- trauma and tragedy

Your own feelings (on the whole)

There are some psychological and medical conditions, illness and injuries that can cause problems with feelings but on the whole it's up to you. If you can accept that you cause your own emotions, you can change them by changing your unhealthy or unhelpful beliefs. Your problems are mainly because of your emotions. It is those that are disturbing you or those that keep you stuck that you need to change.

The intensity of your disturbed feelings depends on how forcefully you hold dogmatic and demanding beliefs. The intensity of your healthy but negative feelings depend on how strongly you hold your desire or prefer-ence belief.

The stronger your 'must' belief, the more intense unhealthy negative feelings, like anxiety, will be. The stronger your 'I want but I don't have to' belief, the stronger your healthy negative emotions, like concern, will be.

Both types of feelings can be extremely uncomfortable so you need to de-velop resiliency and strength to tolerate the discomfort and not give up.

Your own behaviour and performance

If problem behaviour is affecting you or someone in your family, you may need to seek medical intervention. For most of us, however, because our behaviour is also caused by our beliefs, we are responsible for how we behave.

Your performance will be influenced when you face difficulties and chal-lenges. For example, if you have an interview to go to but receive some tragic news, your performance would be affected. It would be totally understandable if you chose to postpone your interview.

Like the process of changing your thoughts and feelings, changing your behaviour can be uncomfortable. You need to develop resiliency and strength to tolerate this feeling in order to achieve your desired goal.

Your thoughts

On the whole, the thoughts that cause your emotions are caused by your beliefs. In the previous chapters you learned how to challenge and change different types of thought. Thinking is habitual and, as you know, chang-ing any habit or pattern is uncomfortable, so developing resiliency and strength will help you to tolerate any discomfort.

Outside your control
Other people

How other people feel and behave is up to them and is outside your control. You cannot control what other people say, do or feel. You are responsible for your behaviour and how you talk to others and they are responsible for their response and their behaviour towards you. You can, however, learn to influence other people by first looking at your own behaviour and your own communication skills.

Some people behave passively in the face of aggressive behaviours, and this passivity is their responsibility. They may tolerate aggressive behaviour for their own reasons, for example, anxiety and fear or simply pragmatism. It is their own belief systems that cause their behaviour.

No matter how skilled you are at communication, other people are outside your control. Accepting that other people are outside your control and that they can do, say and think as they wish can be challenging and uncomfortable. Developing resiliency and strength will help you to tolerate this feeling.

Certainty in everything

You may have beliefs which demand that you be certain before you can allow yourself to make a change or do something new. Unhealthy beliefs about certainty, just like unhealthy beliefs about control, are very common. They are also very unhelpful to you.

Unhealthy beliefs about certainty – which is different from likelihood – need to be changed because they will stand between you and your goal. It's important to accept that risk is part of life. There is always a risk (or chance) that something can go wrong, for you or for anyone. You cannot totally eliminate risk in order to have absolute certainty that everything will work as you want it to. If that is your goal, you will be waiting a long time and not living your life freely. You will know if you have unhealthy beliefs about uncertainty because they will cause you to feel anxiety and behave in an avoidant way. You can minimize risk and increase certainty to a point where you feel able to act, which will vary depending on how risk averse you are. In these situations you need to consider the consequences, but remember the saying 'no risk, no reward'.

Changing beliefs that demand certainty and no risk can feel uncomfortable, and you need to develop resiliency and strength to tolerate this feeling.

Resources for resiliency

Meta emotions

It is very important to develop resiliency and strength to help you tolerate the feelings of discomfort so that you can make a change. You can disturb yourself about any feelings you may have, whether they are healthy or unhealthy.

You have been learning how to change unhealthy beliefs that stand between you and your goal. You've learned that the process of changing unhealthy beliefs into their healthy versions is uncomfortable and may feel strange because you are effectively changing the habit of unhealthy beliefs. You may also disturb yourself about the feeling of discomfort itself, feeling anxious about your unhealthy anxiety or anxious about your healthy concern.

This feeling about another feeling is called a meta emotion. It's effectively having a problem about a problem or a problem about a challenge. Meta emotions play a significant role in resiliency. You know now that change feels uncomfortable, and part of the change process is tolerating this discomfort and pushing through it rather than giving up.

If you have a problem about uncomfortable emotions or about discomfort then you will have an unhealthy belief about discomfort. It means you will be making a demand not to feel uncomfortable or for change to feel comfortable.

Typical unhealthy beliefs about discomfort will be as follows:

- I must feel comfortable when I start something new because I cannot stand feeling uncomfortable; feeling uncomfortable is horrible.
- I must not feel any discomfort when I am doing anything because I cannot tolerate feeling discomfort – it's awful.
- I must feel totally calm and relaxed when I do anything; feeling nervous or anything apart from calm is horrible and I cannot cope.
- I must feel confident when I decide to do something because I cannot bear feeling unconfident – it's awful.
- I must feel confident when I start anything new because if I don't it proves I'm useless.
- I must feel confident when I strive for my goals because if I don't it means I'm useless.
- I must not feel any negative emotions when I do anything related to my goals because if I do it's unbearable.

All the above beliefs are dependent on feeling comfortable, and you know that any change will naturally feel uncomfortable. The problem with demanding change to be comfortable is that it will only cause you to have a lower tolerance of discomfort. You will be oversensitive in relation to feelings of discomfort, which is quite the opposite of resilience.

Healthy beliefs about comfort or discomfort

I want to feel comfortable when I start something new, but it doesn't mean I must feel comfortable, because I can stand feeling uncomfortable even if I don't like it. Feeling uncomfortable is not horrible, it's just bad.

I do not want to feel any discomfort when I am doing anything but I accept that I might. I can tolerate feeling discomfort even if it's hard; discomfort is bad but not awful.

I'd like to feel totally calm and relaxed when I do anything but I accept that I might not. Feeling nervous or anything apart from calm is not horrible, it's just bad and I can cope with it even if I don't like it.

I'd like to feel confident when I decide to do something but it doesn't mean that I must feel confident. I can bear feeling unconfident even if it's hard at first. Feeling unconfident is bad but not awful.

I'd like to feel confident when I start anything new but I accept that I might not. Feeling unconfident does not mean I'm useless. I'm fallible and my worth does not depend on whether I feel confident or not.

I want to feel confident when I strive for my goals but I accept that I might not. It doesn't mean I'm useless. I'm fallible and I remain worthy whether I feel confident or not.

I'd really like to not feel any negative emotions when I do anything related to my goals but I accept that I might. Feeling negative emotions can be challenging but I can bear that and cope with it.

Having healthy beliefs about feelings of comfort and discomfort will increase resiliency and strength because they allow you to accept that you can cope with difficult emotions. They also help you understand that change is naturally uncomfortable. This does not mean that discomfort should be avoided or that it's a sign that you are doing something wrong. It feels uncomfortable when you start to change your beliefs, thoughts, behaviour and start taking action, but this is good because it means you are going through the process of change and being resilient. However, if you begin to find the level of discomfort too overwhelming, it means you have an unhealthy belief about it and you need to apply the CBT process to change it.

The current CBT process for goal achievement is as follows:

Understand the principle of emotional responsibility (Chapter 1).

Understand what emotional health is all about (Chapter 2).

*Set a **SMART** goal (Chapter 3).*

Identify the unhealthy beliefs that sabotage your goal achievements (Chapter 3).

Identify the healthy beliefs that support your goal (Chapter 3).

Identify the 'what's in it for me' reasons for keeping unhealthy beliefs (Chapter 3).

Identify the 'what's in it for me' reasons for strengthening healthy beliefs (Chapter 3).

Understand that tension is part of the change process (Chapter 4).

Identify any obstacles that you may become aware of once you start the above process and develop strategies to overcome them (Chapter 4).

Rehearse your goal, healthy beliefs and the healthy 'what's in it for me' reason (Chapter 4).

Develop other cognitive skills (Chapter 5):

Identify your negative self talk, negative automatic thoughts and hot thoughts.
Identify your constructive self talk, helpful thoughts and healthy thoughts.
Rehearse your goal, healthy belief, and 'what's in it for me' reasons as well as your self-talk, helpful and healthy thoughts.
Be forceful and energetic about your rehearsal.
Use imagery and other emotive and vivid methods when you rehearse.
Keep repeating.

Broaden your self-talk skills (Chapter 6).

You can now begin to apply the above process to develop and strengthen your resiliency.

Example

Sally has been working on changing her unhealthy beliefs because she wants to start her own business. She has been finding it extremely hard to tolerate the feeling of discomfort when she imagines and rehearses her healthy beliefs about taking action in relation to her business plan. She knows that she needs to tolerate this feeling and do it anyway but she finds any feelings of discomfort or tension overwhelming. She realizes that she has a problem with negative emotions and tension, so she sets herself a mini goal of overcoming this problem and learning to become resilient. She applies the CBT process of goal achievement as follows.

Work out your goal about the feeling of discomfort:

- I want to be resilient and strong when I'm experiencing discomfort or setbacks. I want to achieve this change in three months. I want to tolerate discomfort and keep my focus on my goal.

Identify the emotion you feel about being uncomfortable:

- Anxiety about the feeling of discomfort when I'm applying my goal strategies.

Identify the unhealthy belief you have about the feeling of discomfort:

- I have to feel comfortable when I'm applying my goal strategies; I can't stand feeling uncomfortable.

Identify the healthy belief you would like to have about the feeling of discomfort:

- I'd like to feel comfortable when I'm applying my change strategies, feeling uncomfortable is challenging but I can stand it.

Work out your 'what's in it for me' reasons for keeping your unhealthy belief about the feeling of discomfort:

- It stops me from applying my goal strategies.

Work out your 'what's in it for me' reasons about strengthening your healthy belief about the feeling of discomfort:

- It helps me to achieve my goals.

Work out if there are any obstacles that stand between you and your goal of resiliency and develop a strategy to overcome them:

- Urgency to make the change, and accepting that it takes effort and some time.

Rehearse your goal, healthy belief and 'what's in it for me' reasons:

- Reading them and rehearsing them daily.

Reflect on your different thoughts about discomfort and resiliency, i.e. self-talk, negative automatic thoughts and hot thoughts:

- Self-talk: I'm so impatient.
- Negative automatic thought: this is so hard, I can't do it.
- Hot thought: I can't stand this.

Identify the constructive self-talk about discomfort:

- I used to be impatient but I'm learning to be patient and tolerant about effort.

Identify the helpful thoughts about discomfort:

- It's challenging but I can do it.

Identify the healthy thoughts about discomfort:

- This is difficult but I can bear it.

Recite and rehearse your goal, your healthy belief and thoughts about resiliency. Be forceful and energetic about it.

Go through this process twice a day.

Use imagery work if you find it helpful

Imagine that you are getting on with taking action even though you feel uncomfortable. This will help prepare you for tolerating the discomfort when you come to face your challenges.

Challenges are temporary

If you think back to any difficulties or challenges you have experienced you will find that most of them have been temporary. When you experience such a challenge it 'feels' like it will last forever and you just want it to be over. This is understandable because you experience a lot of discomfort. You now know, however, that if you seek comfort in all things, you won't do much and then even that begins to feel uncomfortable.

You have the ability to learn from difficult experiences, setbacks and failures. You can learn to improve your skills and adopt healthy beliefs, so challenges are temporary because you can do something constructive about them. You can get up and have another go but this time you have learnt that:

- A challenge or a setback is not the end of the world, it's just bad.
- A challenge or setback is hard and frustrating but not unbearable.
- You remain a worthy but fallible person who can learn to do it better the next time.
- You learn that a setback or a challenge is a temporary hurdle.

Metaphoric imagery about resiliency

Emotive imagery that's relevant to the healthy belief and goal is not only effective in promoting change but it also helps your motivation. Imagery work can be either specific and realistic or metaphoric. The important thing is that the metaphor is relevant to the change process.

Metaphors have been part of meaningful human communication and storytelling for thousands of years. Sometimes a metaphor encapsulates an explanation in a very vivid and profound way. Children's stories are full of metaphors because they can be understood in childhood. For example, you can metaphorically describe the concept of 'hope' by saying that 'spring always follows winter'. You can imagine yourself in the winter when the weather is cold and wet but sooner or later spring arrives and you see subtle bursts of colour, budding plants and sunnier days.

Metaphors need to appeal to you so that you can use them emotively and vividly. A metaphor with imagery needs to trigger a positive emotional response in you for maximum effectiveness. Start thinking how you can depict resiliency in a metaphoric way with you at the centre of it. What images and pictures does the word 'resiliency' conjure up in your mind? What would you be doing in this metaphoric image of resiliency? The important thing is that it's meaningful to you and triggers a strong, positive emotion.

There are many ways that you can depict resiliency in a metaphoric image.

Mountain metaphor

For example, you can imagine that you are climbing a mountain because at the top is something that you want or an object that you treasure. You start at the bottom, climbing some way and then slipping back, climbing some more and slipping back. You keep imagining yourself getting up and starting to climb again. You are sweating and out of breath from the effort, but you keep on, and you keep climbing back after each slip. You imagine that you are focused on getting to the top of the mountain and then, finally, you imagine yourself there, smiling and raising your hands up to the sky.

Boulder metaphor

This time, you are pushing a big, heavy boulder up a hill. Don't ask why, it's a metaphor. You imagine falling down and slipping back all the way to the beginning, getting back up again and starting to push the boulder back up the hill. You repeat the image of slipping and starting again until you eventually imagine yourself making the final push, the boulder is on top of the hill and you are sitting on top of it looking very pleased with yourself.

100 metre hurdle metaphor

Or you can imagine that you are running a 100 metre hurdle. You imagine yourself falling down from crashing into the hurdles and tripping, getting up and going towards the next hurdle. You fall at some but get up and jump over others, with a determined look on your face, focused on getting to the end. Finally you imagine breaking through the finish line with your hands up, a winner.

Think of your own metaphoric image for resiliency and imagine overcoming setbacks whilst remaining focused on your goal.

Positive imagery technique for developing resiliency

You can use imagery to trigger positive emotions that enable you to desensitize any overwhelming feelings of discomfort you may have during the change process or when you experience a setback. Using positive imagery can help you to cope by triggering positive feelings to counteract the discomfort. Both the overwhelming and the positive emotions are represented by different images. Both images are triggered by imagining them at the same time, or by imagining them fusing together. This technique should be used when you rehearse the healthy belief about discomfort; recite your healthy belief about discomfort or resiliency, and then imagine fusing the image associated with the overwhelming feeling of discomfort to the image associated with positivity.

1. Write down your goal and healthy belief about resiliency.
2. Sit or lie down.
3. Close your eyes.

4. Breathe in deeply, hold it for three or four seconds and then breathe out gently. Repeat this five or six times.

5. Imagine that you are drifting off to your own favourite place of relaxation where you feel most at peace. This could be a place you know well, a place you have read about or a place you have dreamt of.

6. Imagine yourself at your favourite place and let the feelings of relaxation happen naturally.

7. Create an image of the overwhelming feelings of discomfort you experience and put it to one side of your mind.

8. Recall a time when you have felt very relaxed, calm and at peace. Imagine that this is happening to you right now. Let the feelings of calm and relaxation flow through your body as you visualize this memory.

9. When you feel very relaxed, recall the image that represented the overwhelming feelings of discomfort.

10. Rehearse your healthy belief about resiliency.

11. Let the image that represented the overwhelming feelings of discomfort drift to the back of your mind.

12. Remember a time when you felt confident and in control. It doesn't matter how long ago it was; just recall the memory, where you were at that time and what was happening.

13. Imagine yourself in this memory of confidence and control as if it is happening to you right now.

14. Let the feelings of confidence and control grow.

15. When these positive feelings are vivid, recall the image that represented the overwhelming feelings of discomfort.

16. Rehearse your healthy belief about resiliency.

17. Put the image that represented the overwhelming feelings of discomfort to one side of your mind.

18. Recall a memory when you felt very amused and laughed a lot.

19. Imagine yourself in that funny memory and recall who was there and what happened.

20. Imagine yourself in that funny memory as if it is happening to you right now.

21. Let the feelings of laughter grow inside you.

22. When you feel amused, bring to the forefront of your mind the image that represented the feelings of discomfort.

23. Rehearse your healthy belief about resiliency.

24. Let your mind go blank and then imagine yourself back in your favourite place of relaxation.

25. Rehearse your healthy belief about resiliency and imagine yourself dealing with the setback, focused on your goal and actions.

26. Tell yourself that you will now open your eyes and that you will be back in the present, feeling good and whole.

27. Open your eyes.

You can also record these instructions on an audio machine and follow them by listening and imagining.

The above technique is really about desensitizing you to unhealthy meta emotions. If you are anxious about discomfort, for example, this technique will help you overcome your anxiety about uncomfortable feelings and help you to increase your tolerance. For maximum effectiveness use it while rehearsing your healthy belief about discomfort.

Cognitive disputing skills

Cognitive emotive triggers are words or statements that you can use to trigger positive feelings whenever you experience an emotional challenge or setback. When this happens, some form of 'sticking plaster' technique may come in handy, like a cognitive 'pick me up'.

It is important to remember that these techniques are a short-term measure, and any long-term change needs to come from working on your beliefs. Cognitive emotive triggers can take the sting out of emotional challenges and setbacks that you face in the short term.

You've learned about rehearsing and imagining yourself as a resilient person before you encountered any setbacks. You know now how to increase your tolerance to negative emotions and tension while going through the process of change. These techniques helped you see yourself as someone who is strong and bounces back from setbacks. The cognitive emotive triggers are about triggering a positive feeling when you encounter the setback. You will not feel the full intensity of the positive emotion because you will be feeling discomfort from the setback and challenge. At the same time, you can expect the negative emotion to feel less intense. Your ability to tolerate the setback and to bounce back will increase or, to put it another way, if you mix a bowl of hot water and a bowl of cold water, you have warm water.

You can learn how to do this by associating your positive feelings with a word, an image and a feeling. You start by triggering your positive emotions and then associate the emotional state to the word and the image you have chosen. You repeat this process a few times to reinforce the association. Once you have set the cognitive emotive trigger, all you need to do whenever you feel an emotional challenge, or experience a setback, is to repeat your trigger word and quickly flash the image in your mind. This triggers the emotion that you have associated with the word and the picture.

How would you want to feel if you were to experience a setback? The best 'sticking plasters' are feelings of calmness and confidence. You then think of a picture or image to go with feelings of calmness and confidence. You can also think of a colour that for you relates to calmness and confidence. Then finally you think of a word or statement that is meaningful to you. You can think 'resilient and strong', or you can think 're-silient and calm', whatever words or expression are most suitable to you. Once you have thought of these three things, words, image and feeling, you can follow the instructions below:

1. Sit or lie down.
2. Close your eyes.
3. Breathe in deeply and hold it for three or four seconds and then breathe out gently. Repeat this five or six times.
4. Recall a time when you felt calm and confident.
5. Imagine yourself in that time when you had feelings of calm and confidence.
6. Allow these feelings of calm and confidence to grow inside you until you feel them.
7. Keep the feelings of calm and confidence and intensify them in your own way.
8. Open and close your eyes quickly.
9. Imagine or visualize your new picture or colour that depicts calmness and confidence and repeat your trigger word or statement, e.g. 'I'm resilient'.
10. Repeat your trigger word or statement four or five times in a forceful and energetic way.
11. When your feeling of calmness and confidence decreases, open your eyes.
12. Repeat from 1 to 11 twice more.

Now you have a 'sticking plaster' to use whenever you experience an emotional challenge or setback, but please remember that this is a quick, short-term technique. If you feel stuck in the emotional challenge or setback, it means you have an unhealthy belief and you then need to do the more in-depth work of changing it as outlined in Chapters 3 and 4.

Disputing

Disputing is a cognitive skill that involves questioning both your unhealthy and healthy beliefs to prove that the unhealthy beliefs are untrue, illogical and unhelpful to you and that your healthy beliefs are true, logical and helpful to you. You will learn to use this skill to help you tolerate the tension you feel as you move towards your goal and when you experience a setback, to stop you from sabotaging your goal and giving in. Disputing in itself does not enable a shift in your emotions but it does motivate you to work to change them.

What do you dispute?

You dispute the four unhealthy or irrational beliefs that are triggered when you experience discomfort or a setback, and you find yourself stuck as a result. As noted previously, the unhealthy belief about discomfort or setback may not include the four irrational beliefs so you dispute the unhealthy beliefs that apply to your situation. You will recall that the four unhealthy beliefs are:

- 'Must' or 'have to'
- Awfulizing
- Low frustration tolerance
- Self-/other-damning

After you dispute your unhealthy belief about discomfort or a setback, your next task is to dispute the healthy counterpart beliefs, namely:

- Preference
- Anti-awfulizing
- High frustration tolerance
- Self-/other-acceptance

What is disputation based on?

Disputation is usually based on three major arguments. The first is evidence that your unhealthy belief is inconsistent with reality. According to CBT there is no evidence to support any of the four unhealthy beliefs.

The second disputation argument is based on logic. Using logic, you refer to your healthy belief and ask if your unhealthy belief follows logically from it.

The third disputation argument is helpfulness. You ask yourself to think about the effects of maintaining and believing your unhealthy belief and compare them with the effects of holding and strengthening your healthy belief.

At this point you may find it helpful to go back to Chapter 2 to remind yourself of the reasons why unhealthy beliefs are untrue, illogical and unhelpful and why healthy beliefs are true, logical and helpful to you. What you will learn now is how to apply these three arguments to both your unhealthy and healthy beliefs about discomfort and setbacks.

Go through the following exercise and then answer the disputing questions. Learn the disputing questions by heart because you can then use them whenever you want to challenge any unhealthy beliefs.

Exercise

1. Work out your goal about the feeling of discomfort or about any potential setback. For example, 'I want to be resilient and strong when I'm experiencing discomfort or setbacks. I want to achieve this change in three months. I want to tolerate discomfort and keep my focus on my goal.'

2. Identify the emotion you feel about being uncomfortable or about a potential setback. For example, 'I feel anxiety about the feeling of discomfort or possible setback when I'm applying my goal strategies.'

3. Identify the unhealthy belief you have about the feeling of discomfort or about the potential setback. For example, 'I have to feel comfortable when I'm applying my goal strategies. I can't stand feeling uncomfortable', or 'I must not experience any setbacks because that would prove that I'm useless'.

4. Identify the healthy belief you would like to have about the feeling of discomfort or about the potential setback. For example, 'I'd like to feel comfortable when I'm applying my change strategies. Feeling uncomfortable is challenging but I can stand it', or 'I'd like not to experience any setbacks but I accept that I might. If I do it never means I'm useless. I'm fallible but remain worthy regardless'.

Disputing the DEMAND using evidence

Is it really true that you MUST feel comfort or that you MUST not experience a setback?

Is there a law that states you MUST feel comfort or MUST not experience a setback?

Disputing the DEMAND using logic

Just because you would like to be comfortable or would rather not experience a setback, does it make sense to insist that therefore you MUST feel comfort or that you MUST not experience a setback?

Disputing the DEMAND using helpfulness

How does believing that you MUST feel comfort or that you MUST not experience a setback help you to achieve what you want in the long term?

Is believing that you MUST experience comfort or that you MUST not experience a setback going to help or hinder you in your pursuit of your long-term goal?

Disputing the AWFULIZING belief using evidence

If you awfulize discomfort or setbacks, answer the following questions. Remember that awfulizing means 100% bad or that nothing worse exists.

- Is it really true that it is AWFUL if you do not feel comfortable or experience a setback?
- Is there a law that states discomfort or a setback is the worst thing that can happen to you?
- Is there a law that states discomfort or a setback is so bad that nothing worse could happen?

Disputing the AWFULIZING belief using logic

Just because you find discomfort or a setback bad, does it make sense to conclude that discomfort or a setback is the worst thing that can happen to you?

Disputing the AWFULIZING belief using helpfulness

How is believing that discomfort or a setback is awful going to help you to achieve what you want in the long term?

Is believing that discomfort or a setback is awful going to help or hinder you in your pursuit of your long-term goal?

Disputing the LOW FRUSTRATION TOLERANCE (LFT) belief using evidence

If you have an LFT belief about discomfort or a setback – for example 'I can't stand discomfort or cope with setbacks' – then answer the following questions. Remember, if you take an LFT belief literally it means that you would cease to exist when you feel discomfort or experience a setback.

- Is it really true that you CANNOT STAND/CANNOT COPE WITH/CANNOT BEAR discomfort or a setback?
- Is there a law that states that discomfort or a setback is UNBEARABLE?
- Is there a law of the Universe which states that discomfort or a setback is something you CANNOT STAND/TOLERATE?

Disputing LFT using logic

Just because you find discomfort or a setback difficult, does it make sense to conclude that discomfort or a setback is something you cannot stand or tolerate?

Disputing LFT using helpfulness

How is believing that discomfort or a setback is unbearable or something you cannot cope with going to help you achieve what you want in the long term?

Is believing that discomfort or a setback is unbearable/not something you can cope with going to help or hinder you in your pursuit of your long-term goal?

Disputing SELF-DAMNING BELIEF using evidence

If you have a self-damning belief about discomfort or a setback, answer the following questions. Remember, self damning means that you put yourself down about feeling discomfort or about setbacks.

- Is it really true that you are useless/weak/worthless just because you feel discomfort or experience a setback?
- Is there a law that states you become a useless/weak/worthless person just for feeling uncomfortable or for experiencing a setback?
- Is there a law that states you become a useless/weak/worthless person just because you feel discomfort or because of a setback?

Disputing SELF-DAMNING using logic

Just because you do not feel comfortable or because you experience a setback does it make sense to conclude that you are now useless/weak/worthless?

Disputing SELF-DAMNING using helpfulness

How does believing that you are useless/weak/worthless just because you feel uncomfortable or because you experience a setback help you to achieve what you want in the long term?

Is believing that you are useless/weak/worthless just because you feel uncomfortable or because you experience a setback going to help or hinder you in your pursuit of your long-term goal?

Disputing the PREFERENCE using evidence

Is it really true that you would like to feel comfort or not experience a setback, but you accept that it is possible that you might?

Why is it true?

Disputing the PREFERENCE using logic

Even though you would like to be comfortable or would rather not experience a setback, does it make sense to conclude that it is not possible to always be comfortable and never experience setbacks?

Why does it make sense?

Disputing the PREFERENCE using helpfulness

How is believing that you would like to feel comfort, or that you would like not to experience a setback, while accepting that it is possible that you might experience discomfort, or experience a setback, going to help you achieve what you want in the long term?

Is believing that you would like to experience comfort, or that you would like not to experience a setback, but accepting that it is possible that you might experience discomfort, or experience a setback, going to help or hinder you in your pursuit of your long-term goal?

How would it help?

Disputing the ANTI-AWFULIZING belief using evidence

Is it true that it is bad but not AWFUL if you do not feel comfortable or if you experience a setback?

Why is it true?

Disputing the ANTI-AWFULIZING belief using logic

Even though you find discomfort or experiencing a setback bad, does it make sense to conclude that discomfort or a setback is not the worst thing that can happen?

Why does it make sense?

Disputing the ANTI-AWFULIZING belief using helpfulness

How is believing that feeling discomfort, or experiencing a setback, is bad but not awful, going to help you achieve what you want in the long term?

Is believing that feeling discomfort or experiencing a setback is bad but not awful going to help or hinder you in your pursuit of your long-term goal?

How would it help?

Disputing the HIGH FRUSTRATION TOLERANCE (HFT) belief using evidence

Is it true that you find it difficult but that you CAN STAND/COPE WITH/BEAR discomfort or a setback?

Why is it true?

Disputing HFT using logic

Even though you find feeling discomfort or experiencing a setback difficult or bad, does it make sense to conclude that feeling discomfort or experiencing a setback is something you can stand or tolerate?

Why does it make sense?

Disputing HFT using helpfulness

How is believing that feeling discomfort or experiencing a setback is hard, but not unbearable or something you cannot cope with, going to help you to achieve what you want in the long term?

Is believing that feeling discomfort or experiencing a setback is hard but not unbearable, and is something you can cope with, going to help or hinder you in your pursuit of your long-term goal?

Why would it help?

Disputing SELF-ACCEPTANCE BELIEF using evidence

Is it really true that you are not useless/weak/worthless just because you feel discomfort or because of a setback?

Why is it true?

Disputing SELF-ACCEPTANCE BELIEF using logic

Just because you do not feel comfortable or because you experience a setback, does it make sense to conclude that you are *not* a useless/weak/worthless person?

Why does it make sense?

Disputing SELF-ACCEPTANCE BELIEF using helpfulness

How is believing that you are *not* a useless/weak/worthless person just because you feel uncomfortable or because you experience a setback going to help you achieve what you want in the long term?

Is believing that you are *not* a useless/weak/worthless person just because you feel uncomfortable or because you experience a setback going to help or hinder you in your pursuit of your long-term goal?

Why does it help?

Tips

As a general rule, use the arguments that you understand most easily. You can use just one or all of them. I have found that the helpfulness argument is not only easier to grasp but also seems to work more effectively than the others.

Metaphoric disputing

Metaphoric disputing involves using imagery to prove to yourself that your unhealthy belief about discomfort and setbacks is unhelpful and that your healthy belief about discomfort and setbacks is healthy. Unlike other disputing techniques, metaphoric disputing also enables you to shift your emotions more easily because it is vivid and emotive.

Metaphoric disputing involves using your imagination to create an image of both your unhealthy and your healthy belief about discomfort or setback. The image can be whatever best represents your beliefs. The second step is to imagine yourself in your unhealthy belief, looking at the world through its eyes, then stepping out of it, entering your healthy belief and looking at the world through the eyes of your healthy belief.

In both parts you should feel the emotions triggered by each belief so you can really understand what negative feelings it causes – an uncomfortable state with the unhealthy belief and an empowered state with the healthy belief. Then you imagine burning your unhealthy belief out of your mind as finally you commit to and accept your healthy belief.

The following points outline the technique for using metaphoric disputing.

1. Write down your goal and healthy belief about resiliency.
2. Sit or lie down.
3. Close your eyes.
4. Breathe in deeply, hold it for three or four seconds and then breathe out gently. Repeat this five or six times.
5. Create an image that represents your unhealthy belief and an image that represents your healthy belief about discomfort or a setback.
6. Imagine these two images side by side in your mind.

7. Imagine stepping inside the unhealthy belief image as you recite it in your mind.

8. Become aware of how you think and feel and how you see yourself with the eyes of your unhealthy belief.

9. As you recite your healthy belief about discomfort or a setback imagine stepping out of the unhealthy belief image and stepping inside your healthy belief image.

10. Become aware of how you think and feel as you see yourself with the eyes of your healthy belief.

11. Imagine stepping out of your healthy belief image.

12. Imagine burning the unhealthy belief image until no trace of it is left.

13. Imagine drawing the healthy belief image and then recite 'this is the new me now'.

14. Open your eyes.

Repeat this technique daily to strengthen your resiliency.

You have now learned how to prepare and plan for seeing yourself as resilient and strong. If you have followed all the exercises, you have done enough mental preparation and in the next chapter you will learn about taking action.